Prayers for People in Prison

PRAYERS
FOR
PEOPLE IN
PRISON

WILLIAM NOBLETT

OXFORD UNIVERSITY PRESS

1998

Oxford University Press, Great Clarendon Street, Oxford OX2 6DP

Oxford New York

Athens Auckland Bangkok Bogotá Buenos Aires Calcutta
Cape Town Chennai Dar es Salaam Delhi Florence Hong Kong Istanbul
Karachi Kuala Lumpur Madrid Melbourne Mexico City Mumbai
Nairobi Paris São Paulo Singapore Taipei Tokyo Warsaw

and associated companies in Berlin Ibadan

Oxford is a registered trade mark of Oxford University Press

Published in the United States
by Oxford University Press Inc., New York

British Library Cataloguing in Publication Data
Data available
ISBN 0–19–145675–6

1 3 5 7 9 10 8 6 4 2

Typeset in Dante
by The Spartan Press Ltd.
Printed in Great Britain
on acid-free paper by
Bookcraft, Midsomer Norton

This too I know—and wise it were
If each could know the same—
That every prison that men build
Is built with bricks of shame,
And bound with bars lest Christ should see
How men their brothers maim.

Oscar Wilde, *The Ballad of Reading Gaol*

FOREWORD ▓

I F my first few years as Archbishop are anything to go by, during my time I will write many forewords and reviews. I doubt, though, whether I will ever come across a book as brilliant and disturbing as this work by William Noblett. Brilliant, because the work presents a series of snapshots which, put together, catch prison life in its entirety. Disturbing, because as the jigsaw pieces fit together and present a whole picture, the reader begins a chilling descent into a world to which most of society would like to turn a blind eye.

The accounts are not lurid, with only the basic factual detail supplied. This ploy, of letting the reader's imagination unleash the full story, makes for interactive rather than passive reading, so that by the end of the book you do truly sit with those who minister in prison. What could be a very bleak work is redeemed on two counts. First, William Noblett is unashamed of his own humanity and frailty, and that honesty comes through as a shining beacon. Secondly, each brief account ends by moving naturally into prayer, very appropriate prayer, which draws magisterially from old and new.

This is a practical book, born out of a sensitive ministry in the prison service, one in which I was privileged to 'share the cure' during my time as Bishop of Wakefield, and now once more as Archbishop of York. It is a piece of writing I will often return to during my very different ministry, both for the accurate picture it gives of the prison world, and also for the insight it offers to the world which pretends to be far beyond prison walls. I am certain you will find it similarly invaluable, deepening your awareness of God 'in prison, his hideout in flesh and bone'.

✠ *David Ebor*
Archbishop of York

ACKNOWLEDGEMENTS ▒

THE invitation from the Chaplain General to Her Majesty's Prisons to write this book came as a surprise. So too, the time from its conception to its birth, three years. In some ways, however, it has been formulating during my ministry in prison over eleven years and reflects a collaborative style that I have tried to practise during that time. It falls short of my hopes in that I was unable to get as many contributions from colleagues as I would have liked. The exposing of one's vulnerability, theology, and prayer is not for all. I offer my thanks to those who did feel able to contribute, verbally or in writing, and who gave of themselves and their time in so doing.

In addition to those who contributed directly, a number of people helped to bring the book to fruition. Graeme Simmonds, a governor at HM Prison Norwich, who checked the text for accuracy as it reflects the prison context; Malcolm Braddy, Chairman of the East Anglia District of the Methodist Church, my tutor for two years, who kept a watchful eye on my theology; David Fleming, Chaplain General to Her Majesty's Prisons, who asked me to write the manuscript, and agreed the final text; Nigel Lynn at OUP, who kept me on track. All of them offered practical comments, suggestions, and encouragement.

During the three years it has taken to bring the book to publication I have also been studying for an M.Th. in Applied Theology. The preparation of essays, a dissertation, and of this manuscript has taken a huge volume of time, personal and family. I would not have completed either without the active understanding, love, and support of my wife Margaret, and our son Andrew. I owe them much more than lost time.

Nick Wall and Ron Tasker have been my Governors at Norwich and Full Sutton Prisons respectively during my writing time. I express my gratitude to each of them, and to my chaplaincy colleagues, for their willingness to facilitate my absences and to understand my pre-occupation.

All of the stories within this book are based on real situations, real people. Details, however, have been changed or obscured where necessary to preserve the identity of any individual. Statistics, where they have been used, are drawn from a wide range of sources. As ever they are capable of more than one interpretation, and are constantly changing. Absolute accuracy cannot be guaranteed.

I dedicate this book to all who live and work within our prisons and with whom I am privileged to share life and ministry.

I acknowledge with thanks permission from the following to use and/or quote from their work:

Material from the *Alternative Service Book 1980* is copyright © The Central Board of Finance of The Church of England 1980 and is reproduced by permission.

Rob Barr-Thomson, *Healthcare*

The Reverend Philip Berrigan

Dietrich Bonhoeffer, brief extract from *Life Together* © HarperCollins, San Francisco, 1975

The Bourne Trust, *'Prisoners' Week Prayer'*. By permission of the Prisoners' Week Committee

British Council of Churches, adapted from a prayer published in *Week of Prayer for Christian Unity* 1990. Used with permission. *Called Together*

Ben Butler, *Education*

Paul Cavadino, statistics from *Race and Criminal Justice* (Race Matters)

Dr Andrew Coyle, *Prison Numbers Throughout the World*

Crown Copyright material is reproduced with the permission of the Controller of Her Majesty's Stationery Office: brief extracts from *Prison Statistics Publications*; *A Draft Strategy for Health* (1996); *A Report by John Hutchings, HM Inspector of Probation 1996*; *Prison Service Annual Reports and Accounts 1994/95 and 1996/97*; *Prison Disturbances 1990, Lord Justice Woolf*; the *Prison Service Lifer manual*; *Prison Service Recruitment Brochure 1998*; and *Report of the Review of the Role of Boards of Visitors, 1995*

John & Bernie Davis, *Victims* (SAMM-East Anglia)

Brian Dodsworth, *A Brief History of Prison Chaplaincy*

Alan Duce, *International Links Among Prison Chaplains*

Julia Flack, *Living with Risk*

The Venerable David Fleming, Chaplain General, HM Prison Service Chaplaincy

Cathy Green, *Vulnerability*

The Reverend J. R. Hargreaves, *The Word Across the Prison World*

Michael Hollings and Eta Gullick, from *It's Me, O Lord*. By permission of McCrimmon Publishing Co. Ltd.

The Reverend Canon Eric James, *Praying for People in Prison*

The Reverend T. M. Johns, Assistant Chaplain General, HM Prison Service Chaplaincy (*Baptism/Prison Litany Welcome the Stranger*)

The Bishop of Lincoln, the Right Reverend Robert M. Hardy, *The Influence of Religion in Prison*

The Reverend Dr L. M. McFerran, *The Word Across the Prison World*

Sister Elaine MacInnes, OLM, *Light Behind Bars*

Suzanne Moore, extract from an article on Myra Hindley first published in the *Independent*. By permission of the author.

NACRO, *Mental Health Advisory Committee Policy Paper 4*

Penal Affairs Consortium, *Race and Criminal Justice*

The Reverend Canon Keith Pound, *Wholeness and the Therapeutic Community*

Prison Reform Trust, extracts from *Restoring Relationships* and *Into the Dark Tunnel*

Sir David Ramsbotham

Pierre Raphael, from 'The Chaplain's Prayer for Breath' from *Inside Riker's Island* © 1990. Used by permission of Orbis Books

The Relationships Foundation, statistics from *Relational Justice: A new approach to penal reform 1991/2*

Religious Society of Friends in Britain Quaker Social Responsibility & Education (QSRE), extract from *Repairing the Harm (Restorative Justice)*

Fran Russell, Assistant Director of The Howard League for Penal Reform, extract from *Lost Inside—the imprisonment of teenage girls*

The Reverend Bill Salmon, *Confidentiality*

R. S. Thomas, from *Later Poems 1972–1982* (Macmillan). Used with permission

Dr David Wilson, Lecturer in Criminology, University of Central England, *Evil*

Brian Wren, extract from 'I come with joy' from *Piece Together Praise* © 1971, 1995 Hope Publishing Company for the USA, Canada, Australia and New Zealand and Stainer & Bell Ltd, London for all other territories.

CONTENTS ▣

V. Connected Groups 213

INTRODUCTION ▓

The public conscience would be far more active if the punishment of imprisonment were abolished and we went back to the rack, the stake, the pillory, and the lash at the cart's tail . . . It would be far better (for the offender) to suffer in the public eye; for among the crowd of sightseers there might be a Victor Hugo or a Dickens, able and willing to make the sightseers think of what they are doing . . . The prisoner has no such chance . . . the secrecy of the prison makes it hard to convince the public that he is suffering at all.

EORGE BERNARD SHAW, with some exaggeration and in a different age, has, none the less, caught something of current views in at least two respects. First, the public mood and attitude towards those who have committed crimes is very punitive, and many would favour a return to the spectacle of corporal or even capital punishment. Secondly, the continued rise in the number of people being sent to prison, often in what seems to be a case of 'first resort', rather than as a 'last resort', means that 65,771 people are now imprisoned in England and Wales. The Prisons Minister, in early 1997, promised a further 8,600 prison places by March 2000. The Home Secretary, in November 1996, announced that it would cost the taxpayer some £14.5 billion pounds to build enough prison places to cope with the anticipated increases. At the beginning of 1998, predictions by the Prison Service indicate that there may be between 83,000 and 92,000 people in prison by 2005.

Most prisoners will be released back into the community, at some time. The figures put England and Wales near the top of the European league table for imprisonment. The number of people on remand, and therefore unconvicted of a crime, has increased from 12 per cent to 21 per cent, accounting for some 12,000 of those in prison.

Even now, at a time when there have been endless television

programmes, fictional and factual, newspaper and magazine articles, there is still a part of the prison world that is hidden from our view, and is secret. Part of the reason for this secrecy may be a fear that we will discover something of ourselves in those in prison. In the words of newspaper columnist, Polly Toynbee, 'Exploring the outer limits of human evil, we peer into our own dark souls and pleasurably frighten ourselves with our potential for sin.'

Part of this book is an attempt to bring the secrecy to light through the stories of individuals, and to bring to view something of the ministry of chaplains, and others, in a complex, emotional, and sometimes violent, environment.

R. S. Thomas, one of the finest poets of this century, and a priest, reminds us of the need to seek God in unexpected places, one of which is prison:

> 'We ransack the heavens,
> the distance between
> stars; the last place we look
> is in prison, his hideout
> in flesh and bone.'
>
> (R.S. Thomas, 'The Prisoner')

This book has its primary location in 'the flesh and bone' of the lives of people in prison. Most of the pieces take the form of narratives, based in fact, but with some details changed to preserve the identity of individuals. Where possible the narratives reflect 'primary' and narrative theology; that is, theology that arises from the pastoral cycle of human experience and story, becomes reflective theology, and is then given expression in the language of prayer. As will be seen in the narratives, my concern is for the individual within the 'total institution' (Erving Goffman, *Asylums*, Penguin, 1961) which makes up the prison community. In a very limited way I have sought to make connections to other disciplines, notably psychology, and particularly as it provides insight into pastoral issues. Poetry and literature also help. I have sought to 'connect' the stories of individuals with the divine story, with God's story of relationship with us. Elie Wiesel, who suffered in the concentration camps of Auschwitz and Buchenwald during the Second World War, wrote that 'God made man because he loves stories'. In my writing, and in encouraging others to write, I have tried to provide stories that open a door into a space where we can search for something of the divine action in the lives of some difficult people, and in ourselves.

In a sermon to prison chaplains, the German theologian Karl Rahner explored how we might find Christ in prisoners, but also how we might find ourselves in them (*Mission and Grace*, vol. iii, Sheed & Ward Stagbooks, 1966). He wrote, 'We find ourselves in the prisoners when we see in them the hidden truth of our own situation. The truth that we are sinners; the truth that we are self-seekers; the truth that in a thousand different ways, crude or subtle, we are always trying to serve God and ourselves . . . We may be free in a bourgeois, legal sense: we may be responsible for our actions, not only in the sight of men but also in the sight of God . . . But if we have not been set free by the Spirit of God . . . we are nevertheless helpless and hopeless prisoners in the prison of our guilt, our unsaved condition, our inability to perform any saving act.' He goes on to say, 'When you go from your own surroundings into a prison, you do not go out of a world of harmony, light and order into a world of guilt and unfreedom: you stay where you have been all the time. It is merely made clearer to your bodily sense what has been surrounding you all the time.'

The book reflects the concerns of finding God, and finding self within the community of God in prison. Few of us can do that alone, and I am pleased that a number of my colleagues, chaplains, other staff, and a number of prisoners, have felt able to contribute to narratives, or to submit their own. The stories contain the potential to transform us through prayer, and to change our understanding of God. Kenneth Leech has put it like this, 'At heart prayer is a process of self-giving and of being set free from isolation. To pray is to enter into a relationship with God and to be transformed in him' (*True Prayer*, Sheldon Press, 1980, 6).

The book is not intended to provide some sort of theological legitimacy for a system which is constantly stretched to its capacity, with increasing problems and decreasing resources, and whose purpose and sense of direction can easily be lost in the responses forced upon it, but seeks to provide, in part, a prophetic and ethical challenge to Christians, through providing insight into the prison world, by applying theology and highlighting particular situations.

At a time when the Chief Inspector of Prisons, Sir David Ramsbotham, is warning of 'the danger signs that overcrowding and the evil of inactivity are doing real damage to all the progress that has been made over the past 4–5 years', and when the Archbishop of Canterbury, Dr George Carey is calling for a 'reappraisal of the purpose of imprisonment', it seems apposite.

The book reflects the way in which I seek the support of sympathetic and supportive individuals and groups in my prison ministry. Through the book I hope to encourage Christians to understand something of what is being done in their name, and to seek their prayerful support.

The book is not intended primarily for prison chaplains, or for those who live or work within our prisons. Many of them will know more about prisons than I ever will, but I hope if they do read it, they may find it useful. It is intended as a resource book for concerned Christian people, who want to know more, and who may sit and pray with us who minister, in their name, in prison. The narratives and prayers may be used in private, or in public, though some will be too long for public use. The prayers are not prescriptive. People may feel free to use them in whatever way they wish, to adapt them, discard them, or incorporate them in some form into their own prayers. Some of the narratives may form an introduction to issues, which could be used within a discussion group, or Bible-study group.

In the 1564 Scottish Book of Common Order, the congregation is reminded of the need for offenders to be reconciled to God and to the Church, after repentance and the offering of satisfaction or reparation to the victim and the Church. The congregation is asked to embrace the offender as a brother, identifying with his situation. In addressing the penitent, the minister says, 'we all repute your fall to be our own; we accuse ourselves no less than we accuse you; now, finally, we join our prayers with yours, that we and you may obtain mercy.'

'We join our prayers with yours.' The identification, perhaps with reluctance and pain, of our humanity and fallenness with that of the offender is deeply rooted in our Christian tradition, and here, given formal liturgical expression, it conveys a deep theological truth about our need to hold each other in prayer.

As far as I am aware, there is no comparable book available to people anywhere. It is the result of the generosity of all those who have contributed, and of all those who live and work within our prisons. Despite signs to the contrary, God is here, present and active in the lives of many people. Most of the time, however, he has to be sought out. Through this book we can do that together, and perhaps in so doing, be transformed.

PRAYING FOR PEOPLE
IN PRISON ▩

JOHN had been a popular Civil Servant, a good boss in his place of work. He had been conscientious, worked hard, enjoyed his own company, and his home environment. He was articulate, interested in music, especially classical. He read widely and had a good knowledge of English literature. Always ready to discuss his current reading, he was an avid follower of world events. Over many weeks we sat together and talked at length.

Eric too, had worked hard over a number of years. Single, and lonely, he had persevered with his education programme despite failing health. Finally, he obtained the Bachelor of Science degree in Sociology and Psychology, which he so wanted. He constantly gave me papers to read. Abstruse and academic, devoid of 'plain English', I found them demanding. In hospital, he asked me to pray with him as he prepared for his death.

On the face of it, both men had much in common with many others in the population. Eric's request for prayer would seem reasonable under the circumstances. His victims, however, were just a few years older than my young son. Boys whose lives had been 'snuffed'* out by a man whose quest for sexual gratification was uncontrolled.

John was a serial killer. His killings had been in double figures. Reviled by the media, he was greatly feared within the prison. His crimes offended me deeply.

When Eric asked for my prayers, and when I sat in a cell in the Segregation Unit with John, I had to draw deeply on the well of my compassion, my understanding of prayer, and of God. Why pray for, and with, these men? Surely such people are beyond redemption, cannot be offered salvation, do not deserve our compassion? Such questions are frequently directed to me, and I regularly ask them of myself. In my heart I feel I know the answer, but my intellect is hard pressed to give a justification, even to myself.

With both men I was often reduced to silence, unable and unwilling to articulate the depth of my revulsion for their crimes. Whilst I could separate the 'sin from the sinner' in my mind, my heart was telling me something very different. Sometimes I wanted to respond by shouting my incredulity, my lack of understanding, and my pain for those who had died. In private, my thoughts and prayers became a silence and a shouting, as they frequently do.

In the book, *It's me, O Lord*, by Michael Hollings and Eta Gullick (Mayhew & McCrimmon, 1972), there is a description of prayer which I have found useful in helping me to pray:

The important thing about prayer is that it is almost indefinable. You see, it is: hard and sharp, soft and loving, deep and inexpressible, shallow and repetitious, a groaning and a sighing.

A silence and a shouting, a burst of praise digging deep down into lonelinesss, into me. Loving. Abandonment to despair, a soaring to heights which can be only ecstasy, dull plodding in the greyness of mediocre being— laziness, boredom, resentment.

Questing and questioning, calm reflection, meditation, cogitation. A surprise at sudden joy, a shaft of light, a laser beam. Irritation at not understanding, impatience, pain of mind and body hardly uttered or deeply anguished.

Being together, the stirring of love shallow, then deeper, then deepest. A breathless involvement, a meeting, a longing, a loving, an inpouring, a drowning, a swooning, more.

I think prayer is almost indefinable and the more I seek to pray, particularly prayers of intercession, the more difficult I find it to articulate what it is I am doing. And the more I find it hard to do so, the more I am thrown back on the love of God. I know God's love for me as an individual, with all my failings, and through the knowledge of his love for me I know of his love for others, without exception. It is not possible for me to say that God loves some and not others, that he loves the righteous and not the sinner. 'I have come to call not the righteous but sinners' (Mark 2: 17b). It is the certainty of the unconditional love and the unmerited grace of God which enables me daily to enter into the lives of those who are considered by many in society to be 'beasts and perverts, monsters, maniacs, serial-killers, thugs, brutes, hooligans, junkies, parasites', and worse.

'We love because he first loved us' (1 John 4: 19). In the example of Jesus, the Christ, in his compassion for those on the margins of society, cast out by society, made the scapegoats, there lies a call to us to take the pain, the hurt, the oppression, the brokenness, and the brutalization of prison seriously and to say it cannot be accepted as the norm, that it is abnormal and unacceptable for us, who are made in the image of God. It is this, perhaps, to which Oscar Wilde alludes in his Ballad of Reading Gaol, quoted at the beginning of this book. Wilde also wrote, 'The prison system—a system so terrible that it hardens their hearts whose hearts it does not break, and brutalizes those who have to carry it out no less than those who have to submit to it' (Richard Ellman, *Oscar Wilde*, Hamish Hamilton, 1987, 454). This echoes the words of a former Conservative Party Government Minister who said that 'prison succeeds only in making bad people worse'.

I have to acknowledge my part in that brutalization, as one whose representative presence as a Christian priest lends some form of legitimacy to the prison system and all it stands for, and because it has had a profound influence on my personal life, and that of my family. Prison has led me to be much more suspicious of people, to be more critical, less tolerant, more short-tempered with my family than they could ever deserve. Reflections of the social and environmental influences, the expectations of the prison environment they may be, but they exact a high price.

Ironically, it is because of my ministry in such a place, with all its effects, personal and professional, and the painful questions which it asks of me, my faith, my understanding of God, that I discover, and acknowledge my dependence on God. Philip Berrigan, an American priest imprisoned for his opposition to his country's involvement in armed conflict, wrote about what had helped him to remain free in prison: 'I have discovered two things about prayer since entering prison: first that when I pray humbly and honestly I can hack this life even at its bitterest. When I don't pray, I cannot. When I don't pray I begin to apply to life the only power I really know—violence. Inch by inch I begin to disintegrate, and so do my relationships with others. I begin to brood about the injustice of this experience, and the dark side of my soul assumes control. But when I pray I accept my dependency on God and on my friends. And a love not my own is lent me. And I can continue.'

Philip Berrigan wrote as a prisoner, but I fully concur with his words and his experience. Why do I stay in prison ministry? Because it is here that I need God more than anywhere else. Alexander Solzhenitsyn, reflecting on his time of incarceration in Russian Gulags, said, 'Bless you prison . . . for it was there that I discovered that the meaning of earthly existence lies in the development of the soul.'

The unmerited grace of God, so much a part of the gospel proclaimed by St Paul is rooted in the concept of the unconditional love of God. The word 'grace' comes from the same root as gracious and graciousness, virtues which, one might think, are often lacking in prison. And yet, I can say with confidence, 'But God proves his love for us in that while we were sinners Christ died for us' (Romans 5: 8). In that act of love, I can identify and accept a gift freely offered and for which I have done nothing, nor which I deserve, or have in any way earned. In my gratitude I turn to prayer, and in my ministry I strive to reflect something of that unconditional love and unmerited grace in an environment which is often contemptuous of the notion of love, and of God.

I frequently use one of the prayers suggested at the conclusion of the Alternative Order of Confirmation included in the Prayer Book as proposed in 1928. In its more modern translation it reads:

> **Go forth into the world in peace;**
> **be of good courage;**
> **hold fast that which is good;**
> **render to no one evil for evil;**
> **strengthen the fainthearted; support the weak;**
> **help the afflicted; honour everyone**
> **love and serve the Lord,**
> **rejoicing in the power of the Holy Spirit.**

(Based on 1 Thessalonians 5: 13–22)

In starting this chapter I deliberately portrayed some of the positive aspects of John and Eric's lives. I was being selective about their good points, as I could so easily identify the bad points. I do not want to ignore the bad, or to emphasize only the good. It does not mean ignoring their crimes, the sins which they have committed, but it does mean continuing to show them 'respect, esteem, reverence, or worth', as the *Oxford English Dictionary* defines 'honour'. The Christian belief in God the creator means that nothing we do can entirely mar his image in us. No matter how hard I have found it to do so, I have always sought 'to find that of God in everybody' as the Quakers say. The Christian writer, Virgil Georghiu, in a piece much quoted by prison chaplains has written:

The police seek in every human being a murderer;
the wise man and the philosopher seek in every murderer a human being.
We Christians seek God in every person . . . even in murderers.
And each of us will find what he seeks:
the police will find their murderer;
the philosophers will find their human beings;
and we, we shall find God in every person.'

(Quoted by Little Brother Peter in Jesus Caritas, 58: 33)

I believe that in 'seeking God in every person' honour can be accorded in a similar way to the way in which Jesus honoured those whom he met. In his dealing with the woman taken in adultery (John 8: 1–11), he is gracious towards her, according her respect as a human being. In a sense he 'honours' her, at a time when many would have been calling for a harsh sentence.

When he tells the remarkable story of the Prodigal Son, or, more properly, the Loving Father, he makes it clear that he gives honour to the returning son as a gift, despite all that has gone before. He nowhere suggests there are some actions, some situations from which it would be impossible for the son to come home. Nor is there any suggestion of rejection by the father because of anything which the son may have done. It is a dramatic story about repentance and forgiveness, both of which are central themes in Luke and Acts. The son acknowledges his wrongdoing and says he is not worthy, and in so doing he receives a deep and undeserved kindness, the unmerited grace of the Father. The honour we accord to each other is a mark of our understanding of the honour God freely gives to us. For me, this idea is summed up in one of the prayers for use after communion in the *Alternative Service Book*:

> **Father of all, we give you thanks and praise, that when we were still far off you met us in your Son and brought us home. Dying and living, he declared your love, gave us grace, and opened the gate of glory. May we who share Christ's body live his risen life; we who drink his cup bring life to others; we whom the Spirit lights give light to the world. Keep us firm in the hope you have set before us, so we and all your children shall be free, and the whole earth live to praise your name; through Christ our Lord.**

The declaration of love, the giving of grace, the wonderful symbolism of God in Christ, meeting us and bringing us, the undeserving and sinful, home, is powerful. In all of these instances the compassion of Christ and the experience of salvation are intimately linked, even where the person who is offered salvation is unable to make restitution for his offences.

One of the criminals crucified with Jesus (Luke 23: 33–43) receives the promise of paradise in the hour of his death, without any opportunity to lead a new life, or to make restitution. Only Luke records the words of that repentant criminal and the response of Jesus '. . . today you will be with me in Paradise' (Luke 23: 43). Whilst the words 'forgiveness' and 'salvation' are not used, they are implied in Jesus' words. And as Jesus is crucified we hear him pray for the forgiveness of those who were crucifying him: 'Father, forgive them; for they do not know what they are doing.'

In the parable of the tax-collector and the Pharisee (Luke 18: 9–14), God answers the prayers of the tax-collector and not as Jesus' listeners would have anticipated, those of the Pharisee. As far as we know, this minor tax-collector was not involved in reparation and those who heard Jesus must have been overwhelmed by the implications of this sort of story. Later, we see salvation for the chief tax-collector, Zacchaeus (Luke 19: 1–10) as Jesus takes the initiative and invites himself to his house, and into his transformed life.

In the parable of the Good Samaritan (Luke 10: 25–37), the most unlikely of people performs an extraordinary act of compassion. Such stories were, and are, radical and alternative teaching and they are at the very heart of Christian understanding. It is clearly seen in the way Jesus is portrayed as someone who brings the outcast, the stranger, the enemy, the betrayer, home and gives each one a place at the banquet of God's reign.

In one of his collections of sermons, *Judge Not*, Canon Eric James (Christian Action, 1989) speaks on the text 'Honour everyone. Love the family of believers. Fear God. Honour the emperor' (1 Peter 2: 17). He says: 'To me, perhaps the most moving scene in the whole New Testament is when Judas comes with a crowd, with swords and staves, and betrays Jesus to them with a kiss. What does Jesus say to his betrayer? Does he *dis*honour him? Does he refrain from honouring him? He says to him: "Friend, wherefore art thou come?" The commentary on that verse in the beautiful fourteenth-century book of mystical German writings *Theologica Germanica*, is: "He said to Judas when he betrayed him: 'Friend, wherefore art thou come?' Just as if he had said: 'Thou hatest me, and art mine enemy, yet I love thee and am thy friend.' As though God in human nature was saying: 'I am pure, simple Goodness, and therefore I cannot will or desire or rejoice in, or do anything but goodness. If I am to reward thee for thy evil and wickedness, I must do it with goodness, for I am and have nothing else.'" That is to me the very basis of honouring not just good people, whoever they may be, but *everyone*.'

Canon James, as Preacher to Gray's Inn until 1990, was regularly preaching to many involved with the law; judges, barristers, solicitors, law students, and his exposition of what it means to 'honour everyone' has had a considerable influence on my thinking over many years. As Christians we are called to the counter-cultural practice of loving our enemies, of praying for those who offend against us, of showing compassion to those in need, of honouring everyone, difficult though it may sometimes be.

Such ideas and practices are often contrary to the way in which society thinks, where hatred and retribution are regularly seen as normal, and even healthy, and where they are occasionally accorded divine sanction. The way of Christ, it seems to me, is the opposite to such a view and it is reflected in prayer for those who most hurt us, in prayer for those in prison, and those imprisoned by their passions, hurts and distorted images of self and others.

'We never feel so good as when we are punishing someone,' said Bertrand Russell. The element of truth in this thought must be acknowledged, but it needs to be challenged by Christian people whose Lord offered a radically different alternative in the example of his love and compassion. In a society which seems increasingly punitive, Christians are called to offer a different approach to the person in prison. I acknowledge the difficulties in any such approach and I don't always find it easy when faced with some of the people I meet, but as Eric James has said: 'We dare not admit defeat in the task of reclaiming and restoring this person and that from whatever evil he or she has fallen into, for our religion teaches us that Christ himself lived and died to reclaim not some sorts of sinners but all sorts.'

NOTE
* 'snuff' films usually show the sexual abuse, torture and murder of young people.

A BRIEF HISTORY OF PRISON CHAPLAINCY IN ENGLAND AND WALES ▨

> Lord, what would become of the prisoner if Christian society, that
> is, the Church, were to reject him as civil society rejects him? . . .
> there could not be a greater despair than that for the prisoner.

FYODOR DOSTOEVSKY had been a prisoner. He knew the depths
of human failing, and developed an extraordinary insight into
the mind and character of prisoners. He lived amongst those
who had committed incredible violence and acts of deprivation. Of his
time in prison at Omsk, he wrote, 'I consider those four years as a time
during which I was buried alive and shut up in a coffin. Just how
horrible that time was I have not the strength to tell you . . . it was
indescribable, unending agony, because each hour, each minute
weighed upon my soul like a stone . . .' The conditions were
appalling, and yet, he says, 'even in penal servitude, among thieves and
bandits, in the course of four years I finally succeeded in discovering
human beings. Can you believe it; among them are deep, strong,
magnificent characters, and how cheering it was to find gold under the
coarse surface . . .'

More recently, echoing the first quote from Dostoevsky, a prisoner
in a maximum security gaol in England wrote, 'Tell my mother that
every prison has a chaplain, and no matter what others say about us,
no matter who may abandon us, the Church never will, and neither
will our Lord. He knew what it was like to be deserted in the Garden.'

In the Licence given by each Anglican Bishop to those priests who
minister within his Diocese, are the words, 'Receive the cure of souls,
which is both mine and yours.' For me, these are powerful words,
bestowing on both parties a responsibility for shared ministry in the
prison context. The Bishop represents the wider Church of which we
are but one part. We who minister in prison have a responsibility to

the Church. Part of what this book seeks to do is to fulfil that responsibility through providing an insight into prison life and into the ministry which it demands. The Church's presence in English and Welsh prisons has been officially recognized since 1773 when an Act of Parliament authorized Justices of the Peace to appoint salaried chaplains to their local prisons. The salary was not to exceed £50 per annum, and was to come from the county rates.

It may be a surprise to some, but up until this time most gaols were privately run, including one or two under the control of Bishops! The profit motive meant that prisoners were charged fees for the services provided for them whilst in prison. In the Fleet Prison, made famous by Charles Dickens, charges were on a sliding scale, with an Archbishop expected to pay an entrance fee of £10! At that time, few were willing to pay for the services of a clergyman, and formal acts of worship took place infrequently. With the introduction of salaried chaplains, the situation slowly changed. Interestingly, the opening of the Wolds Prison in April 1992 brought to an end a period of over one hundred years in which all prisons in the United Kingdom had been directly managed by central government. Private-sector involvement in the penal system had returned.

In the nineteenth century, clergy were at first appointed on a part-time basis and they had a purely pastoral role. In recent times the former Archbishop of Canterbury, Robert Runcie, has reiterated this role. 'In talking to prison chaplains I have emphasised their pastoral role. This is in line with the commission given to bishops, priests and deacons of the Church of England at their ordination, when the pastoral emphasis is overwhelming; they are to provide for the flock and to minister to the sheep who have gone astray.'

The first chaplains attended to the sick and those about to be executed, but some found their task depressing and unrewarding. Complaints arose that such men could not do much in a prison which echoed with profaneness and blasphemy. The same might be thought true today! But ministry is partly about faithfulness, and the continuous and renewed call to be where God's people are, in whatever circumstances.

The office and role of chaplain was given much greater significance following the powerful influence and advocacy of John Howard, whose famous book, *The State of the Prisons in England and Wales*, appeared in 1777. John Howard had visited prisons in Holland where services were regularly held in a prison chapel. Howard urged that similar arrangement should be made in English prisons and he made a plea to gaolers not to hinder prisoners from attending 'divine worship'. Robert Peel's Gaol Act of 1823 gave more careful definition of the responsibilities of the chaplain, and made it possible for the stipend to be as much as £250 per annum.

Between 1816 and 1877, central government had responsibility only for convict prisoners, and when the first of these prisons, Millbank, opened in 1816, the Church's mission with prisoners was given much greater stimulus. In Millbank, which was designed to hold one thousand prisoners, the atmosphere was very different from that which had prevailed in the much smaller, county gaols. The experiment was firmly built on the conviction that evangelism was the answer to crime. The chapel stood at the very heart of the penitentiary and this was to provide chaplains with a unique opportunity. The authorities directed that every prisoner must attend religious services and must behave reverently in chapel. Going one step further, they even made the chaplain the governor of the establishment. He was able to order the programme to suit his avowed aim and all the rules were geared to achieve the object of religious exercises, by which the convicts would be reformed. Each warder (now called Prison Officers), carried a Bible, and was expected to quote Scripture at appropriate moments.

The experiment was not considered a success, however, and it proved that even the coercion of the penitentiary cannot bring about change without a heart which is open to the love of God.

Other prisons were soon to follow at Parkhurst, Portland, and Dartmoor. In 1842, Pentonville Prison was opened. Known as the Model Prison, it was the first of fifty-four prison buildings constructed to a similar design during the next six years, of which most are still in use today. As we have seen so often, the model was taken from the American experience, and transported to England. Essentially a system of solitary confinement for all prisoners, it relied on discipline carried to extreme lengths. It came from Pennsylvania, where faith in the value of solitude as a means of reforming criminals was almost fanatical. Prisoners were placed in cells, and could be shut off from human companionship for many years—a situation still experienced by prisoners in oppressive regimes in some countries, even today. The prisoners stayed in their cells for divine worship, many desperately trying to catch sound of a human voice, with the preacher standing in the corridor. In American 'super-max' prisons, Sunday worship is conducted by television linkage to each cell.

At the time, the deprivation of human fellowship was designed to encourage communion with God. Reminiscent of monks in their cells, it has been suggested that the concept of prison as we know it came from a monograph written by a seventeenth-century Benedictine monk, in which he recommends that wrongdoers be reformed by sampling a spell of monastic life. In the 'model prison' the chaplain's role was a major one. To men desperate for companionship, he was to dispense the consolation of the Gospel.

The task proved to be impossible. Even with an assistant, it was not easy to get around all the cells, and eventually, a compromise was agreed. The prisoners would be taken to chapel on Sundays for worship, but in order to maintain their isolation, they were made to wear hoods over their heads, and to sit in individual boxes during the service, so they could see the preacher, but not each other.

Eventually, this system of solitary confinement, which had partly come about as a protest against the indiscriminate herding of all kinds of prisoners in enforced cohabitation, gave way to one of classification and training, much as we know it today.

The chaplain's role, however, continued to be enshrined in the various Prison Acts, up to and including that of 1952, the most recent. In a sense, the pastoral role of which Lord Runcie spoke has become part of the requirement placed on chaplains through what are called 'Statutory Duties', contained both within the Act, and in various Prison Rules. Effectively, they are what most chaplains would see as being important pastorally as they involve seeing prisoners as they come into the prison (Receptions), and daily if they are in the Segregation Unit, the Health Centre, or the Vulnerable Prisoner Unit.

Additionally, people are seen in their cells, at worship, their workplace, or in groups. No member of the chaplaincy team is limited by that which is defined as 'statutory', and these duties are but the springboard to involvement with the whole life of the prison, in different ways, and at different levels, with prisoners and staff, and their families.

Brian Dodsworth, a former chaplain, and to whom I am grateful for much of the historic material in this piece, describes chaplains as 'standing at the cross-roads of human experience, able to meet with men and women, often in crisis'. Sense needs to be made of their waiting, their pain, and, perhaps, their guilt. Prison represents an extreme human experience, and it is here that people sometimes encounter God, with joy and hope, and occasionally, with a sense of sins forgiven.

The ministry to those in prison will always take various forms, but the purpose must be to proclaim something of the unconditional love of God. It is not about being in a position to moralize, to impose a particular viewpoint. It is about encouraging a process of growth and self-discovery, which may take much time. For many chaplains, they can only 'plant the seed', and hope and pray that it will be nurtured. We have to hold to the conviction that, however desolating an experience it may be, prison can be a stimulus to provoke real choices, and transformation of lives. At the heart of each person who ministers in prison, there is a faith rooted in the reality and purpose of God, in whom all things are possible.

Chaplains are called by God, and by the Church, to a shared ministry in a difficult place. Their task is the joyful proclamation of the love of God, and they are in prison to be used, to be accessible and available to give simple, and, sometimes, costly care. A former Roman Catholic colleague came into my office just days before Christmas. He was just managing to hold back his tears. 'Look at this', he said. It was a Christmas card, given to him by a prisoner, one of his congregation, and signed with his prison number. When Fr. Barrie went to see the man, a lifer, to ask him why he had signed it in this way, he replied, truthfully, 'I don't see myself as a person any more, just as a number.'

Brian Dodsworth writes, 'Unless imprisonment can become part of a journey toward a goal rather than a desert of purposeless waiting, the chaplain's help is of limited value. Endless patience is required to stay present with people who cannot yet choose a road—for, in the end, it can never be chosen for them.'

In the book of Ezekiel, the people of God are in exile in Babylon. Ezekiel's account of his pastoral ministry includes the words, 'I came to them in captivity, and I sat where they sat . . .' (Ezekiel 3: 15). In this book, you are invited to sit with those of us who minister in prison, to share our ministry, but above all, to pray with us.

THE INFLUENCE OF RELIGION IN PRISON ▨

T HE RIGHT REVEREND ROBERT HARDY, the Bishop of Lincoln, is
the Anglican Bishop to prisons in England and Wales. The Bishop
represents the Archbishops of Canterbury, York, and Wales within
the Prison Service, and the views and interests of the Prison Service
Chaplaincy in the House of Bishops. He also speaks on issues related to
prisons, and the criminal justice system in the House of Lords, the General
Synod of the Church of England, and in the House of Bishops. Through the
General Synod, he chairs a sub-group of Synod members interested in prisons
and the criminal justice system. He is a regular visitor to prisons throughout
the country as he seeks to understand what is happening first hand. He
provides support and encouragement to chaplaincy teams, and members of
staff. In the piece which follows, 'Bishop Bob' provides an overview on the
ways in which religion can be an influence in prison, but also raises pertinent
questions about the purpose of imprisonment, and the role of Christians in
helping to give direction.

Christians are involved with those in prison, because Jesus himself
related to prisoners. He was betrayed and arrested; He was humiliated
and accused, and His own family suffered in the agony of his
punishment. That much is clear from the Gospels. What is also clear is
that in His ministry Jesus showed a particular concern for the
disadvantaged and the deprived. He specifically commended those
who visited prisoners.

From the beginnings, then, Christians have been inspired to care for
those in prison. They have interpreted this in a variety of different
ways. Some have been reformers, and in our own country some of the
greatest names in penal reform have been men and women who drew
their inspiration from the Gospels. Others have been concerned to
question the place of imprisonment and much of the basis of our

criminal justice system. Others, again, have sought to value prisoners and to help them towards a good and useful life. It is part of the essence of imprisonment, that it is, for the most part, tucked away, and hidden from the normal commerce of society. But it is a fact that there are an increasing number of prisoners at the moment, and more of us (especially those who call themselves Christian) have to face the issues that those in prison pose. This, too, raises questions for us.

No one can enter a prison without becoming aware that this is one of the extreme environments of life. Here are people deprived of many of those features which make life tolerable—freedom of movement and choice, and restrictions on normal social and sexual intercourse. Prisons are places of constant movement. They are authoritarian and regimented. They bring together the violent, the immature, and the weak-willed. As institutions they cannot avoid creating anxiety and loneliness. Not infrequently they give opportunity to the bully and the pretentious. All this makes ministry in prison a sobering and testing experience. It is front-line work of care, and calls from those who undertake it a considerable degree of self-knowledge and a sure grasp of our faith and personal value and belief.

Think of this a little more. Arrest and reception into prison are traumatic and dehumanizing experiences. Most people in prison need help in coping with the loss of self-respect; in one sense, they lose their identity. They become a number. Their physical conditions are basic and limited, their companionship is enforced, and their life is totally restricted and controlled. Anyone therefore who accords them dignity and worth—in Christian terms those who remind them that they are still children beloved of God—begins to set them on the road to redemption and hope. Most often these qualities are communicated informally and sometimes the most effective pastoral care offered in prison is in casual conversation and informal contact. In doing this, one frequently finds there is a refreshing spontaneity and a direct honesty among prisoners, and anyone who ministers to them needs to have a ready sense of humour and to be alert and sensitive to the opportunities for pastoral contact which the prison system provides.

At the same time, there is a need to balance both a judgemental and an accepting attitude in the face of encounters where often there are strong feelings of anger, guilt, and sin. In my experience, indulgence is rarely helpful here, and frequently the minister or visitor has to make a delicate judgement as to his response. Sometimes a firmer attitude can give the offender some real framework for support. On other occasions an accepting attitude is more advantageous: it encourages confidence and self-awareness. Whatever course is adopted, the aim should always be to help the prisoner accept his situation and understand it in such a way that he himself is brought to pass judgement upon it. Only this new insight can bring real hope and the possibility of establishing a new beginning. Here, again, a firm grasp of theological insight and possibility is an important advantage. One needs to know what one believes and be able to communicate it in simple, direct terms.

Almost all prisoners respond to a good listener. Most of them can tell a good tale, and whereas in prison not all answers are necessarily truthful, there is often a real willingness amongst prisoners themselves to deal with direct and personal questions. Sensitivity on the part of the listener is clearly important, but being alongside the prisoner in a total sense is equally significant. It is not for nothing that in the Scriptures truth and freedom are connected. Nor is it by accident that the prophet Ezekiel in the Old Testament could describe his ministry of pastoral care towards the prisoners in Babylon in terms of listening and standing by. His phrase 'I sat where they sat' can still provide a touchstone for our ministry in prison today.

It should be obvious from all this that there are enormous opportunities for people of faith (especially women and lay people) to work in prisons. All the penal establishments in the country have at least one chapel, usually at the very heart of the prison community. Attendance at worship is always on a voluntary basis, but proportionately, it is often very high in relation to the church attendance of the general population. Of course, it is possible to be cynical about this, but there is no doubt that the worship of a prison creates a real opportunity for giving prisoners new vision and hope, implanting the message of the gospel, and adding immeasurably to the quality of life. Most chaplains would testify warmly to the enrichment of prison worship through the presence of Christians from 'outside'.

When we go into a prison, we go as guests, recognizing the complexity of the institution and the devoted work of its chaplains and prison staff. Denominational labels and ecclesiastical rank in my experience mean very little to most prisoners. Again, in my experience, most prison staff welcome a thoughtful 'outsider' and are always ready to share their own concerns and experience of prison life. They, too, deserve our concern and pastoral support, for the work in prison is often depressing and apparently unrewarding. Equally important is our role as a bridge-builder, an intermediary, going into prison as part of a team of concern, acting in communion with fellow Christians, and members of other living-faith traditions from the locality. It is, I believe, as we do this regularly, thoughtfully, and prayerfully, that we not only begin to care for prisoners and those who work in prison, but also to enrich our own discipleship, and to develop our wider ministry in Church and Society.

The task of a chaplain does not change in its essentials. He or she is called to proclaim God's word, to call sinners to repentance, to baptize, to prepare for Confirmation, to preside at the Eucharist, to lead the people in worship, to teach and encourage them, to minister to the sick and dying. Chaplains are to act as 'messengers, watchmen and stewards of the Lord' (Church of England Ordination Service). They pray for their charges and study the Scriptures, and serve and build up the family of the Church.

That task remains constant. Nevertheless, just as Jesus' ministry was lived out in a particular situation, so is that of the prison chaplain. His ministry shares in its essentials with all other Christian ministries, but it takes from the prison context its outward style and emphases.

Can we sum up the influence of religion in prison? I see the place of religion in three ways: First, it helps the individual to be in touch with God, the source of love and forgiveness for each one of us however we understand it. Loss, spoiling, estrangement, and guilt. These feelings are common to all of us, whether inside the prison system or outside it. Religion brings us face to face with these and with God—the great Giver and Forgiver, and God illuminates our path and gives us hope in dealing with the world around us.

Second, religion helps the individual to be in touch with himself.

Most of us are damaged in one way or another. Some of us have not known love so our feelings are starved and strange and unrecognized by ourselves. Religion can help us face ourselves, it can put us in touch with our feelings and open the door of peace.

Third, religion helps the individual to be in touch with the community. All of us need friendship, acceptance, and understanding. We need the experience of being able to worship with the community of faith and to know ourselves as part of a community beyond the prison and our immediate circumstances. Our religion should give us that and keep the rumour of God alive in our hearts. The prison world is often stark, frightening, inhospitable, but it can give us time and space, and an opportunity to begin again.

––––––––––

Therefore, since we are surrounded by so great a cloud of witnesses, let us also lay aside every weight and the sin that clings so closely, and let us run with perseverance the race that is set before us, looking to Jesus the pioneer and perfecter of our faith, who for the sake of the joy that was set before him endured the cross, disregarding its shame, and has taken his seat at the right hand of the throne of God.   (Hebrews 12: 1–2)

––––––––––

> **When all within is dark,**
> **and former friends misprize;**
> **from them I turn to You,**
> **and find love in Your eyes.**
>
> **When all within is dark,**
> **and I my soul despise;**
> **from me I turn to You**
> **and find love in Your eyes.**

When all Your face is dark,
and Your just angers rise;
from You I turn to You,
and find love in Your eyes.

(Israel Abrahams, based on Ibi Gabriel,
from *The Oxford Book of Prayer*,
ed. George Appleton OUP, 1985, 274)

NOTE
Much of this piece was based on an article which the Bishop wrote for the Chaplaincy
Journal, *New Life*.

PRISON NUMBERS
THROUGHOUT THE WORLD ▦

DR ANDREW COYLE, *the Director of the recently founded International Centre for Prison Studies, at King's College, London, and a former governor of Brixton Prison, has written extensively about the use of imprisonment. In this piece, which formed part of a talk given to prison chaplains in September 1997, he highlights the increasing use of incarceration in the past twenty years. Andrew helps to give an international perspective to my more localized and personal reflections. I have, with his permission, concluded the piece with a quotation by Winston Churchill.*

In the last twenty years there has been a massive expansion in the use of imprisonment across the world. The increase has occurred in democratic countries and in totalitarian states; it has happened in rich countries and in poor; it has happened in countries in the north, the south, the east, and the west.

In the Netherlands in 1975 the rate of imprisonment was 17 people per 100,000 of the population. By the end of 1995 it was 80 per 100,000.

In December 1992 the prison population in England and Wales stood at 40,600. By the end of 1997 it had risen to 63,000 and continues to rise at the rate of almost 1,000 per month.

In 1980 the total number of people in federal, state, and local prisons in the United States of America was 494,000. By mid 1997 it had risen to 1,700,000; that is, over 615 men and women per 100,000 of the population. This rise has been most concentrated in some of the largest states. In 1980 there were 22,500 people in prison in California. In 1996 that figure had risen to 147,712.

The consequences of this increased use of imprisonment have been dramatic. In some countries there has been a concurrent increase in prison places, with massive expenditure on prison building. Other countries have not been able to afford to build more prison accommodation. They have simply crammed more prisoners into the available space. Overcrowding means two, four, ten times as many prisoners in a room as there should be. In extreme cases it means prisoners sharing beds. In these environments it is no surprise that disease raises its head and that violence erupts.

The most extreme example of what appears to be an unstoppable rise in prison numbers is in the United States of America. Between 1980 and 1994 the percentage increase of people in prison in the United States was 323 per cent. More than 11 million men and women pass through America's prisons each year. They are divided unequally on a racial basis. Seven per cent of the population of the United States is made up of male African–Americans. Almost 50 per cent of all men in prison in America are African–American. Out of every 100,000 white Americans, 306 are in prison. The comparable figure for African–Americans is 1,947.

In the United States one out of every three African–American men between the ages of 20 and 29 is either in prison, on probation, or on parole. At least two-thirds of all African–American men can expect in their lifetime to be arrested, gaoled and have a criminal record. The chance of a young African–American coming under the control of some part of the criminal justice system is much higher than his chances of going to college for further education. In 1992, there were 583,000 black men in prison compared to 537,000 in further education.

There are several examples in South America of what happens when a massive increase in the prison population is not matched by an increase in resources. In Judicial Unit 40, a detention centre in Bogota, Colombia, in 1995 cells were often so full that prisoners were forced to lie on top of each other. Up to nineteen prisoners were crammed into cells designed to hold four.

The Modelo Prison is the main pre-trial prison for Bogota. It has a capacity for 1,500 prisoners. In May 1995 it held 3,450 male prisoners. At any one time there are about 150 guards to look after these men, a hopelessly inadequate number to effect proper supervision. Most of the guards are in their late teens and serving their year of compulsory national service. The prisoners are held in five large accommodation blocks built around patios. In each of these units there is a prisoner who is nominated as 'monitor'. This in effect means that prisoners have developed their own rules and regulations for running the patios. Prisoners who cannot pay or who do not have influence with the lead prisoners are likely to fare very badly.

In the prisons and penal colonies of the Russian Federation one witnesses the terrible consequences which result when the infrastructure of the State is unable to support a massive increase in its prison population. In 1991 the average number of prisoners in pre-trial detention was 157,000. The Russian Ministry of the Interior estimates that the average for 1996 will be 320,000. It is estimated that there are 1.2 million people in prison in Russia. In 1995 the prison population rose by 42,000. Official predictions estimate a rise of 50,000 in 1996. Conditions are worse in the pre-trial prisons, known as SIZOs. It is not uncommon that up to ninety prisoners will be squashed into a room officially meant to hold twenty prisoners. The room will have forty beds.

Addressing a parliamentary hearing in Moscow in October 1995, General Yuri Kalinin, Head of the General Penitentiary Department, said, 'I have to confess that sometimes official reports on prisoners' deaths do not convey the real facts. In reality, prisoners die from overcrowding, lack of oxygen and poor prison conditions . . . Cases of death from lack of oxygen took place in almost all large pre-trial detention centres in Russia . . . The critical situation in the SIZOs is deteriorating day by day: the prison population grows on average by 3,500 to 4,000 inmates a month.'

Following a visit to Butyrskaya and Matrosskaya pre-trial prisons in Moscow in 1994 Professor Nigel Rodley, United Nations Special Rapporteur on Torture reported, 'The Special Rapporteur would need the poetic skills of a Dante or the artistic skills of a Bosch adequately to describe the infernal conditions he found in these cells.'

Some of the worst prison conditions are to be found in countries which are former British colonies. The Nigerian Civil Liberties Organization reported that in 1991 there was significant overcrowding in most of the country's prisons. The two largest prisons in the country had overcrowding of 72 per cent and 190 per cent respectively. Zaria Prison, with space for 120 prisoners, held 646; that is, overcrowding of 438 per cent. A prisoner in Zaria described what this overcrowding meant in practice:

We have three batches in my cell, and I am in Number Two. Other cells have four, even five, when there are many prisoners. When it is time to sleep, we all make space for the first batch. We stand at one end of the cell, or sit. Only the first batch lies down. After four hours, they get up, and we lie down to sleep. After four hours, we get up, and the third batch will sleep.

The mood and temper of the public in regard to the treatment of crime and criminals is one of the most unfailing tests of the civilization of any country. (Winston Churchill, 20 July 1910)

I
PRISON LIFE

RECEPTION ▨

I n 1995, 125,654 persons were received into custody. Approximately 70 per cent of prisoners are aged 16–34 years, and 1.3 per cent are over 60 years, compared with 35 per cent and 25 per cent respectively in the general population. Each one will react to the transition in slightly different ways, but the central experience is similar for all.

Fred was 43 years of age when I met him in the Prison Health Centre. Though not a Christian, he had asked to see me. 'I never believed I would ever experience anything like it,' he said. 'It was awful. The reception officer said to me, "Who are you?" "Mr Taylor," I replied automatically. "No you're not," came the immediate reply, "You're Taylor FA26704." It was at that moment that I really felt the full force of being inside'.

Fred described the way in which his few possessions had been searched, his wallet emptied, the photographs of his wife and children carelessly handled. That simple action caused him deep pain. As we talked he reflected on his time in police cells, in the van bringing him to prison, known as 'the sweat-box'. When it had entered the first of the prison gates the engine had been turned off whilst it was security checked and the appropriate paperwork about its 'contents' were given to the Gate Officer. Before it restarted and before it entered the inner gates, Fred said his heart had raced as he viewed razor-wire and high fences from the tiny window of the van. He asked himself, 'When will I next go out?'

He had never been in prison before and now he was being 'processed', subjected to a 'strip-search' which he saw as the final humiliation as he was 'dehumanized', stripped of his dignity. 'I felt as if I was being mocked,' he said, 'though no one said a word wrong. The whole procedure just seemed designed to humiliate me. I know it's the system but it's awful.'

After mocking him, they stripped him of the robe and put his own clothes on him.   (Matthew 27: 31*a*)

- - - - - - -

> Crucified God
> you know what it is to be mocked,
> to be stripped and vulnerable.
> Be with those who
> enter prison for the first time today.
> Be present in their vulnerability
> and in those who have care of them.
> In this vulnerability may they
> know their worth in your eyes.
> In their anxiety and uncertainty
> may they know that your Son has
> shared their experience and
> transformed it.

I had a letter from Jean, a former prisoner, in which she described the sense of loss of identity which she experienced on entering the prison system. She also wrote of the healing which subsequently took place and of the eventual knowledge of God's love and acceptance of her. She wrote:

'I can remember the lack of emotion that surrounded me on entering the reception area of the Prison, the expressionless faces and hard voices that "greeted" me at a time when I most needed to feel acceptance, understanding, and warmth. Up until then I had not been so much aware of the "universal" rejection of me as a person, but this realization was a hard revelation of the fact that I, from that moment, ceased to be a person. I had become a number, a number that would be etched in my memory forever.

' "Go into the cubicle and take off your clothes," I was instructed by one of the duty reception officers. "You can put on the dressing-gown there, and call us when you're ready." Without feeling I followed the instructions. The dressing-gown was rough and cold, but as it had no belt with which to tie it, I wrapped it tightly around myself, waiting for what was to come next. "Take off the gown and do a twirl." I did. The officer came right up close to me and said, "Open your mouth." As I did this she felt through my hair and then looked into my mouth. "Right," she said, "put the gown back on, pick up your clothes and follow me." I entered behind the officer into a well-lit room, furnished with a large desk, filing cabinets, and weighing scales. Two large chairs were situated at either end of the desk. "What is your name? Date of birth? Your religion? Your nationality? What are you charged with?" and many more questions. I answered without thinking, as if it really wasn't me who was speaking, and then, "Your number is PN46570. You must remember that number. You will have it as long as you are in this prison and you will be identified by it throughout the prison."

'Who am I? I thought. Am I really this criminal, this nobody?

'Having had a bath I was led to my cell and the door slammed shut behind me. Alone and afraid I thought some more. Am I really who they say I am? Why can't I remember the person I thought I was? I don't know who I am any more.

'I really continued in this "zombie" state for some time, searching for answers, which, I was to discover, only God could provide.

'Over time, and in my emptiness, I turned to the God from whom I had turned away for so long. I knew he could hear me, that he was listening and whilst there was no "flash of lightning", no "instant change", I knew God had welcomed me to Him. There, in the stillness, I began to learn of the person God intended me to be rather than the person I thought I should be. Never before had I been so much aware of the fact that I was a Child of God, chosen by Him, and that it was only through my ignorance, my selfishness that I had chosen to deny Him.'

O Lord, you have searched me out and known me.
Where can I go from your Spirit?
How weighty to me are your thoughts, O God!
　How vast is the sum of them!
I try to count them—they are more than the sand;
　I come to the end—I am still with you.

(Psalm 139: 1, 7, 17, 18.)

For you did not receive a spirit of slavery to fall back into fear, but you have received a spirit of adoption. When we cry, 'Abba! Father!' it is that very Spirit bearing witness with our spirit that we are children of God, and if children, then heirs, heirs of God and joint heirs with Christ—if, in fact, we suffer with him so that we may also be glorified with him. I consider that the sufferings of this present time are not worth comparing with the glory about to be revealed to us.　(Romans 8: 15–18)

Jean's prayer:

Ever living, ever loving Lord
your mercy, love for, and knowledge of me
is so too great for me to understand.
But your promises that you
will hear us when we cry out to you
are so true.
I thank you that you are always there,
ready to reach out to us in a way that
only you can.
May we come to know you more and more,
to know of your wonderful plans
for our lives, and by this may
we truly come to be new creations,
seeking to do your will, rather than our own.
Lord, in your name we pray.
Amen.

Jean is now a Pastoral Assistant in a parish.

SEPARATION ▨

E RIC sat with a cup of coffee in his hand, dejected. The realization of the consequences of his offence and its effect on his family had begun to hit him and he had sought a place of refuge, in the quiet of the chapel.

Unlike an estimated 43 per cent of male prisoners who had lost their partners since the start of their prison sentence, Eric still had the support of his wife and children. Perhaps, not surprisingly, some 66 per cent of prisoners have children, with as many as 100,000 children experiencing the imprisonment of their fathers in any year. As many as 40 per cent of fathers serving sentences receive no visits from their children. Sometimes, of course, the truth of the situation is kept from children, to protect them, and as part of a coping mechanism by some parents.

Eric's acknowledgement to me, and to his family, of his guilt, had caused him much embarrassment. He could see in his wife and children their embarrassment and the feelings of conflict which they experienced on entering the visits room. Joy at being with Eric, shame at being in such a place.

In conversation, he said, 'I knew what I was doing, but I never realized the effect it would have on those I love.' Eric's wife and children were innocent victims, of his actions, and of a system in which innocent and guilty are punished alike. The now popular refrain, 'If you can't do the time, don't do the crime', ignores and trivializes the devastation which comes to many families, and it ignores the centrality of relationships, impinging on the future of all concerned. Too many become scapegoats in their communities and relationships may break under the strain. Children, lacking the stability which they need, may suffer emotional damage, providing a basis for future behavioural problems, and, potentially, for entry into crime or delinquency. Resentment, mistrust, and fear of authority is almost inevitable, for some.

Eric, six months on, finds himself still 'trying to explain myself to my family, always apologizing, and always fearful I will lose them. Sometimes I find visits so hard that it would be better not to have them at all—the emotional trauma, concentrated into one hour, three times a month, is unbelievable—it takes days to get over them . . . God knows what it's doing to my wife and children.'

I have known some prisoners, particularly those imprisoned for 'life', who have found the burden of guilt and separation so intense they have broken family ties, in the hope of coping more easily with their time inside. Such a decision involves enormous 'cost' for them and for their families.

Release, and reintegration can also be a traumatic time, and without the right form of support, all too many reoffend.

> **God of love,**
> **the pain of separation**
> **often overwhelms**
> **and is destructive.**
>
> **We hold in your presence**
> **all who are separated**
> **in mind or body from**
> **those whom they love,**
> **and especially the 'innocent victims'**
> **of imprisonment, the families,**
> **friends and relatives of prisoners.**
>
> **We acknowledge before you**
> **the importance of relationships,**
> **with one another,**
> **and with you.**
> **Enable us to pursue them,**
> **for their good,**
> **and in response**
> **to your pursuit of us.**

WAITING ▨

'I'M celebrating an anniversary today, chaplain,' said the prisoner as I walked past him. I stopped. 'What's that for, then, Nick?' I asked. 'I've been here a year today.' I could hardly believe it. For me, his time had seemed to pass so quickly. 'When's your trial?' I asked. Despondently, he gave me a date five months in the future. 'Yeah, I'll have done seventeen months before I even get into court.'

He went on to express his anger and frustration with a judicial system which was moving so slowly and in the process was causing him deep distress, anxiety, and uncertainty. And his family as well. He was contemplating taking some form of action to highlight his situation and he wanted to know if I felt hunger-strike would be a way of bringing his case to the fore. I tried to dissuade him on the grounds that he would ultimately hurt only himself and his family. 'I don't care,' he said, 'I'm dying inside anyway.'

The year had certainly taken its toll. His appearance had altered. His complexion was sallow, having had little time in the fresh air and sunlight. His eyes were deep within their sockets. His face was unshaven and his voice flat. He had been waiting for twelve long months. Now he knew another five had to be endured. No words of mine could help Nick. To have spoken about the spirituality of waiting, or the need for 'patience' would have been to insult him.

Some weeks before in the prison car-park, I had met Pete. He had been released from court on the second day of his trial. He had waited one year and two days on remand. In court, his case was dismissed by the trial judge, who said it should never have come to court. He spoke movingly of his 'waiting', and of what he had lost; his wife, his children, his home, his business. Because of a conviction some years before he would not be eligible for compensation. His bitterness was understandable. His determination to rebuild his broken life admirable.

Such lengthy periods of time spent waiting on remand are rare, but not exceptional. It is hard to see how they can further the cause of justice and I am pleased that recent legislation in Parliament will enable positive changes to be made to reduce the time prisoners are held on remand prior to coming to court, particularly in view of how many subsequently receive a non-custodial sentence.

———

> Therefore justice is far from us,
>   and righteousness does not reach us;
> we wait for light, and lo! there is darkness;
>   and for brightness, but we walk in gloom.

(Isaiah 59: 9)

———

**God of justice
help us to be alert
to your presence
in our lives.
Help us to understand
that waiting is not passive,
but active and open-ended.
We pray for patience,
for the ability
to stay where we are,
to live each situation to the full
in the belief that something hidden
will be revealed to us.
We hold before you those
who are impatient
and always expecting
the real thing to happen somewhere else.
May we dare to stay where we are
that we may know your presence
in the present moment.**

BARGAINING ▨

THE phone call was from a solicitor. Could Tom attend court the following Friday to speak for Roger. He had, after all, undergone a conversion experience. I explained that members of the chaplaincy team rarely attended court to speak in this way. We would be inundated with requests, particularly if people felt that 'a result' would be helped by our presence. In this context 'a result' means a positive outcome for the accused. I said 'no', it was not our policy, as a team, to do so.

A few hours later an eloquent barrister phoned. He understood all that had been said to the solicitor, but . . . he was sure that his client had undergone a life-changing experience and that the judge should be made aware of the difference between the youth (he was just 18) who had committed the offence some months before, and the 'born-again Christian', now transformed.

My colleague, a young volunteer, who was leaving us two weeks later decided to 'break ranks' and to appear in court. He spoke on Roger's behalf, eloquently and with passion.

Two days later I was on the wing, and I asked staff if there was anyone who wanted to attend chapel. I mentioned Roger. 'He hasn't asked,' said one. I was surprised, he had been so regular an attender, Sunday and Thursday. 'He's had a bit of bad news this week,' said another, 'Might be no harm if you saw him.'

I knocked on his cell door, opened it and was faced with a young man who would not speak to me; made it clear I should leave; rejected my presence.

Was he rejecting me as a person, as a chaplain, as a father figure, or the God whom he felt had let him down in court? He had been given a four-and-a-half-year sentence. I was reminded of my young son, who sometimes rejects me when he does not get what he asks me for. It is usually temporary. Perhaps for Roger too.

> Lord,
> we all try it,
> to do deals with you.
> To think belief is
> a 'quid pro quo'.
> Help us not to
> minimize your love
> by reducing it to our understanding.
> Help us to know your love for
> its own sake.

SPACE 🔳

O NE of the foremost prison architects of the eighteenth
century William Blackburn believed that the design of
prisons could help prisoners to self-control and rational
behaviour, leading in turn to a reshaping of human nature. The
concept of the monastic cell, in which the prisoner could contemplate
his offence before God, seek forgiveness and repentance, was strong.
Monks may well have found their cells a place of contemplation, but
for a prisoner it is a place of confinement.

Today such a concept is meaningless for the vast majority of
prisoners and the sense of isolation imposed by a 'single' cell may do
harm to some people if they are unsuited to it psychologically.

Most cells are about 4.0m × 2.6m and designed for one person. In
many prisons it will be shared by two people, two chairs, a small table,
two lockers, a washbasin, and a toilet. A small window, 2 metres from
the ground, gives some natural light and some air, though little when
the door is closed, especially in summer. There is little 'personal' space
in such a cell, in which meals must also be eaten and leisure activities
indulged.

It is both 'personal' space and 'public', for there is constant intrusion
during the day—officers locking and unlocking, other prisoners in and
out, probation staff, chaplaincy staff, and, perhaps, a search team
checking security, looking for illegally held items, including drugs. And
just occasionally, and unannounced, a 'sniffer' dog helping the search
teams.

Ever present, too, is the observation panel in the cell door—the
'spy-hole', the 'eye in the door'.

In such a place the opportunity to respect personal space is limited.
But it can be done, to a limited extent. Whenever I, or one of my
colleagues is going to a cell, despite our carrying cell keys we will

always knock on the door before inserting the key, and, when we open the door, will always ask 'May I come in?' It is the prisoner's 'home' for however short or long a period that might be.

> **Lord God**
> **your Son sought space**
> **to find himself, and you;**
> **space for regeneration**
> **and re-creation; help us**
> **respect the need for space**
> **necessary for each individual's growth.**
> **Help us to encounter**
> **and engage you in that space.**

VICTIMIZATION ▨

I HAVE rarely seen violence perpetrated in my time in prison. I have seen the consequences—the death (mercifully, rare), maiming and scarring, physical and mental, of prisoners and staff. As I sat with Graham, who could only explain the attack as being racially motivated, he showed me the stitches in his skull, caused by the most common of prison weapons, a battery, tin can, or some other heavy object placed in a sock and then swung at the victim from behind and usually aimed at the head.

People are frequently threatened, and an increasingly used weapon to go with this form of intimidation is a syringe full of blood which the victimizer claims to be infected with HIV / AIDS.

A recent study has shown how pervasive victimization is within our prisons, with as many as 46 per cent of young offenders and 30 per cent of adults being assaulted, robbed, or threatened with violence in the month preceding the survey. In 1994/5 the Prison Service recorded 5,760 incidents of assault. It is acknowledged that this may represent only a small number of incidents, as victims do not always report to staff, for fear of retaliation from other prisoners, and a feeling that nothing was likely to be gained. The figures represent, however, a six per cent reduction on the previous year, the first downturn after five years of continuous increase.

The survey identified six types of victimizing behaviour—assault, threat of violence, robbery, verbal abuse / insult, theft, and exclusion from activities.

It is, perhaps, understandable, that such incidents, which are combined with those on staff members, may create a 'climate of fear' from time to time. In response to this problem of victimization/ bullying in prison, a strategy was introduced in 1993 which aims to help staff measure the extent of the problem and to change attitude to it. It also seeks to provide improved supervision and detection of the problem, and to support victims; and to challenge the victimizers to face up to their antisocial behaviour and to change.

Against such a background it could become easy to assume that only force, and, more particularly, violence, is the only effective response and this sentiment seemed to be underlined by a former Prime Minister whose policy of 'condemning more and understanding less', is so at variance with Christian thinking. Christians working and ministering in such an environment have to hold before them the theological possibility of forgiveness in a world where God's grace seems, so often, to be absent, and to seek for alternative models.

Why do you make me see wrongdoing
    and look at trouble?
Destruction and violence are before me;
    strife and contention arise.

(Habakkuk 1: 3)

Lord of life,
in the midst of
a violent world
help us to seek for
an alternative way;
to seek for the way of
peace and reconciliation
which brings about the
transformation of
broken lives.

We hold before you
victimizers who are victims,
broken people who
want to break others,
sad people whose sadness
is in their actions.

Be present in the words
and actions of those
who seek alternatives;
and as we learn to
embody forgiveness
we acknowledge our
brokenness before you.

DRUGS ▨

I T is believed that about 63 per cent of people entering prison have a drug habit of some sort.

The Prison Service has taken active, positive, and successful action to reduce the amount of drugs entering prison. Random drug-testing was introduced in prisons in 1995, and during the financial year 1996/7, 57,500 samples were taken. Of those, 24 per cent were tested as positive. In the year 1997/8, this had reduced to 21 per cent.

Charlie had been tested. He was the last of seven children, but one too many. At two years of age he was in a children's home (it is calculated that about 30 per cent of male prisoners held in 1996 had been in some form of local authority care—about 17,000 prisoners).

He thinks he was about 13 or 14 before he saw his mother again. At about that time he went to live with his father and stepmother. Relationships were strained and within a short time he was involved in petty crime which escalated over a few years, culminating with a sentence in a Detention Centre (now called Young Offender Institutions).

He was introduced to a 'spliff', a joint or reefer of cannabis. Unlike many others, Charlie believes cannabis can lead to harder drugs and that few people are likely to start drugs by using heroin or crack-cocaine.

On release from the Detention Centre he got heavily involved in the 'rave' scene, where the music, the atmosphere, and the incredible 'buzz' which drugs gave, enhanced every experience. Ecstasy, at about £15 a tablet at that time, soon gave way to crack-cocaine at about £20 a 'rock'—a piece about one-fifth of the size of a small, round mint. On average he spent £300–£400 each week, sometimes £1,000.

Burglary and theft paid for this habit and when he was eventually caught he got a three-year sentence. Aged 25, he began to wonder about the direction of his life and he took no further drugs in prison.

Eighteen months later he was on the streets again, penniless, homeless, and 'lost'. Within days he was robbing, within weeks back on hard drugs. He bought a car, rented a flat, gambled more, increased his drug intake, and his dependency. The happiness he sought continued to evade him. Within months he was back in prison, depressed and determined to leave drugs aside.

A childhood interest in religion stemming from his time in the children's home led him to chapel. He acknowledged the mess he was in, the physical and mental anguish which led to him crying himself to sleep for three months, as he 'rocked' himself on his bed. He started reading the Bible and was eventually baptized. He arranged to go to a Rehabilitation Clinic if he got a non-custodial sentence. He did not, and he went down for two years. Moved to another prison he was quickly involved in supplying heroin and crack-cocaine. He started to 'use' once more.

Released again, he decided to put his past behind him and a relative gave him a job, learning to fit windows. 'A bit rich that, really, given that I was more used to removing them!' It was irregular work, with low pay, which led to him feeling he was going nowhere. He sought for alternative work, 'but the more I knocked, the more doors were closed'. His relationship with his girl-friend was a mess. In the midst of it all, he sought out a priest, who talked with him, listened to him, and said, 'You know what you have to do, do it!'

The work stopped, and the bills mounted. On his way to pay for crack-cocaine he crashed his girl-friend's car, causing £4,000 worth of damage. In despair, he spent the last £40 of the housekeeping money on crack. Fearing the response of his girl-friend, he burgled, and was caught. A day later, he arrived in this prison.

Within a short time he stood on a chair in his cell, with one end of a strip of sheet tied to one of the window bars, the other end tied around his neck. A quarter of an hour passed. The despair and isolation which he had felt slowly began to pass. Strength came from somewhere, and a sense of 'calm' entered him. There could be 'no bargains, no promises, just me and what I want to do', he thought.

Charlie has changed. No longer, it seems, does he say to God, 'Here I am, let's hear what you've got to say,' with the expectation of receiving instant answers. Trying again, he has got another place in a different Rehabilitation Clinic. He feels his life is no longer at a crossroads, but facing a one-way street, whose direction he must take. He is, he says, 'more focused, and prison can teach me no more'. He is reading his Bible again, but less intently. As he waits for trial, he is hopeful he will not be one of the positive drug tests.

The recent introduction of 'therapeutic programmes' to help prisoners with drug-related problems is a major initiative within the Prison Service and whilst the rise in illicit drug-taking within and without prison is increasing, a significant contribution is now being made to help those who want help. Therapeutic programmes are available in twenty-two prisons at present, with a further thirty soon to participate.

God of freedom
we hold before you
all who are
imprisoned by addiction
and for whom life has
no meaning except in illusion.

God of freedom
help them to overcome
the fear of self
which holds them hostage.

God of freedom
who sent your Son
to set us free,
strengthen them
by your Spirit
that they may
be able to seek new directions,
be helped to work for their freedom.

Many of those with whom I have contact never find that freedom of which the prayer speaks. Mickey was 27 years old when we first met. He had used drugs for nearly fifteen years. He regularly came and went from prison, and often said he would not live until he was 30. The last time we spoke he had inherited some money, and a new start was predicted as he left, yet again. Within weeks he was dead, from an overdose. Shortly afterwards another two ex-inmates were also dead, from overdoses. Not all will be able to change direction.

> **God of compassion**
> **we entrust to your care**
> **those who have died**
> **as slaves to addiction.**
> **In your mercy**
> **grant them rest.**
> **And in our failing them,**
> **release us.**

BROKENNESS ▨

' Are you High Church?' came the question from Mike as I arrived in the Health Centre to lead the Sunday worship. I tried to explain that prison chaplains really should be 'broad' church, to be flexible and responsive to people's needs, not seeking to impose a personal, predetermined churchmanship on those in chapel.

I enquired about his church background, to be told he had been on the Parochial Church Council, the Deanery Synod, and Diocesan Synod in his home area. In chapel, where it is usually difficult to get men to name one hymn they might like to sing, he could name many, and the names of the tunes! Robust and vocal in the early part of the service, he read the lesson with confidence.

In the prayers I could detect at first, and then saw, the movement of his hand as he wiped away the tears. At the Peace, he seemed less confident. During the Eucharistic prayer the tears continued, intermittently.

At the invitation to communion I improvised on some words I had read by the American liturgist John Westerhoff.

My brothers, I invite you to bring your lives, in their brokenness and incompleteness, but wholly acceptable to God; that he, in this Eucharist might take your life, transform it and give it back to you made whole, transformed with his love.

The tears became more evident as the power of these words, the work of the Holy Spirit, and the turbulent emotions he was experiencing, combined in a deeply meaningful way for Mike. Afterwards, composed once more, he was subdued and reflective, more in touch with his emotions, and with God.

Broken bread has become a very significant symbol in our Christian liturgy. In its symbolism there is a deep sacramental meaning which concerns the acceptance of our brokenness before, and by God. At a more fundamental level it is about the simple sharing of food and drink, the one communal meal in many prisons, where most people eat alone.

In eating broken bread, in drinking wine, we try to become like Jesus, to obey his word and to follow him. Perhaps Mike was rediscovering his calling through the acceptance offered by God, manifest in the Eucharist.

For I was hungry and you gave me food, I was thirsty and you gave me something to drink, I was a stranger and you welcomed me, I was naked and you gave me clothing, I was sick and you took care of me, I was in prison and you visited me.   (Matthew 25: 35, 36)

Lord, in our brokenness
we receive your broken
body in Christ;
broken on the Cross
and repeatedly in the Eucharist.
Take our lives
shattered by experience,
and in transforming them,
help to make them whole.
Enfold us in your
light and power that
your will may be done.

TIME ▓

F OR six months I had responsibility for the chaplaincy in a women's prison, just a few miles from Wakefield Prison, where I was the Anglican chaplain. Twice a week, and every third Sunday I left the high-security environment and went to New Hall women's prison. At the beginning of 1997 women were held in fifteen prisons in England, but none in Wales. Within a total prison population of 65,771 some 3166 are women. The figures reflect a growth of 68 per cent in four years.

It was then a small prison, with just over one hundred prisoners. It has continued to grow. It also has a mother and baby unit. It was, and is, a busy prison with a high turnover of prisoners. They had difficult stories to tell, of sexual and physical abuse, of drug addiction, petty theft, and prostitution. Some were imprisoned for non-payment of fines, particularly relating to TV licences. I do question whether prison is an appropriate place for fine defaulters, of whom I meet many. In Holloway women's prison in London, about five or six women each week come in for non-payment of their TV Licence, and one in twenty is a fine defaulter. At the time of writing, a proposed Crime Bill makes provision for such people to be given a community service order instead of a prison sentence.

In 1966 the number of fine defaulters received into prison was 8,555, less than half of those in 1995, and accounting for about 10 per cent of all receptions, the lowest proportion on record. The number of women in prison who pose a threat to the public is very small.

Jan's story was not typical. She had come from a comfortable protected background. In all she was in prison for nearly eight years. Nothing, she said, could have prepared her for her first experience of prison. Facing a long sentence she expressed feelings of being desperate, hopeless, and lonely, combined with guilt and self-hatred for the pain that she had caused.

Jan sometimes remarked that there were so many others around her who were like her that they never shared their feelings. Each one of us, she said, 'was trapped in our own prison, within the prison around us'.

Jan was not able to share the depth of her guilt, feeling nobody would understand. There had been heavy media cover of her trial and some hostility when she first entered prison.

As time passed she was to come to terms with everyday life in prison, and with what had happened in her life. As she said, she had plenty of time to think, to reflect on a life which seemed to be going nowhere.

It was in that 'time' that Jan eventually decided 'to reach out to God' and in doing so she realized the significance of Christ's life and death. It was a slow process, a gradual conversion but it became the 'most painful and joyous moment of my life', she said when we spoke in the chapel after worship. We had sung the hymn 'Do not be afraid' with its chorus

> Do not be afraid, for I have redeemed you.
> I have called you by your name; you are mine.

For Jan, it gave expression to everything which years of imprisonment, physical and spiritual, had denied her.

> But now thus says the Lord,
> he who created you, O Jacob,
> he who formed you, O Israel:
> Do not fear, for I have redeemed you;
>   I have called you by name, you are mine.
> When you pass through the waters, I will
>   be with you;
> and through the rivers, they shall not
>   overwhelm you;
> when you walk through fire you shall
>   not be burned,
>   and the flame shall not consume you.
> Because you are precious in my sight,
>   and honoured, and I love you.

> (Isaiah 4: 1–2, 4*a*)

Loving Father
we give you thanks
that you have redeemed us
through your love.
Help us to realize
that in the midst of our
loneliness and anxiety
you are at our side.
We acknowledge your presence
and your call which
comes when we listen
for your voice.
We rejoice that we are
your people and you our God.

SENTENCED ▦

'THE Face of Evil', proclaimed the front page of one tabloid newspaper. 'Kinky killer', another. Each accompanied by photographs. 'Girl's killer gets life', the more restrained heading on the inside page of a broadsheet. Standing in Sainsbury's, I briefly glanced through each paper. Significant words leapt from the page, each one powerful in its condemnation of a woman who had murdered.

This was the same woman with whom I had sat the previous Sunday. And with whom I had prayed.

Now, she was starting a life sentence, and I was confused. Confused by what I had read, which seemed so at variance with *who* I had encountered. Some words from William Trevor's powerful novel, *Felicia's Journey*, kept ringing in my ears, 'Lost within a man who murdered, there was a soul like any other soul, purity itself it surely once had been.'

As we had spoken I glimpsed something of that 'lost soul', and in so doing I acknowledged how damaged it was, and yet, how God seemed present, and active, because of that, and not despite it. I could not begin to understand why she had committed the crime, but I tried to begin the process of understanding the person who had done so, through listening, encounter, and dialogue.

As I left her I knew she would get 'life'. Now, in Sainsbury's, the tabloid newspapers seemed to assault her dignity, and mine. And yet, I was left with a feeling that God, the God of compassion and forgiveness, continues to offer a release from our darkness, and can indeed provide the hope of reconciliation and new life, even in the face of sin.

God, whose face
is that of love,
be with those
who have recently
been sentenced.
In their uncertainty
and in their despair,
be present.
Enable their release
from darkness, and
through reconciliation
and hope, to seek
new life and restoration
in you.

We pray for those
involved in the media,
for their responsibility
in reporting news;
that they may do so
having regard for
the value of each person.

NOTE
William Trevor, *Felicia's Journey* (Penguin, 1995), 212.

DOING LIFE ▦

On 30 April 1997 there were 3,523 male life sentence prisoners held in English and Welsh gaols, 83 per cent of whom had been convicted for murder. There were 128 female life sentence prisoners.

The average time served by life sentence prisoners first released on licence has gradually increased from 11.1 years in 1986 to 14.3 years in 1997. It must be remembered that this 'average' relates only to those who have been released and they represent a small proportion of 'lifers'. There are many who have served between fifteen and thirty-five years.

In the twenty-two years up to 1994, 1,691 people were released on 'life licence'. On 'licence' means an offender may be returned to prison automatically if he / she breaks the law, or even shows any cause for concern to the supervising Probation Officer, such as, a change in personality or behaviour, alcohol or drug abuse, or showing signs of repeating the circumstances which may have led to the original offence. Any reasonable cause for concern which may be considered a risk to the public could result in the lifer being returned to prison. A licence is for the natural life of the offender.

Less than a tenth (9 per cent) of the licensees released between 1972 and 1993 were reconvicted of an offence within two years, and the number of convicted killers who kill again remains at about a half per cent.

There are two types of life sentence for adult offenders:
- a mandatory life sentence, which is the only sentence the courts can impose for an adult found guilty of murder.
- a discretionary life sentence, which might be given for a serious sexual, or violent offence where there is no fixed time imposed by the law. Examples would be arson, rape, manslaughter. Such

sentences are usually passed where it is not possible to determine at the time of the sentence whether the prisoner will be safe to release at the end of a determined time. It could also be used to highlight the seriousness of the offence.

The situation is slightly different for Young Offenders, those under the age of 21 years. Four possible sentences may be imposed:

- detention during Her Majesty's pleasure. In effect this is the equivalent to a mandatory life sentence and is the only possible sentence for a person convicted of murder who was under the age of 21 at the time of the offence. Between 1979 and 1994, 210 young people aged 10–17 in England and Wales were convicted of murder and 220 of manslaughter. Over half of these killings were committed by 17-year-olds. Few involved children below the age of 14, who totalled eight convicted of murder and four of manslaughter.
- detention for life, which is the equivalent of a discretionary life sentence. Such a sentence must be used for people over 18, and convicted of offences other than murder.
- custody for life, which is the sentence for a person aged 18 or over, but under 21 at the time of the offence, who is convicted of murder.
- for a person over 18, but under 21 at the time of the offence, and who is convicted of any other offence for which a life sentence may be passed on an adult, the court shall, if it considers that a custodial sentence for life would be appropriate, sentence him or her to custody for life.

The Prison Service, working according to its Statement of Purpose, Vision, Goals, and Values, and in partnership with the Probation Service, seeks to work positively and constructively with those doing life. It does so in a number of ways:

- by allocating them to prisons whose regimes best meet the needs of the individual.
- by helping them to come to terms with their offence.
- by assisting them to identify, address, and modify their problem behaviour and attitudes.
- by ensuring their suitability for release is objectively assessed by staff in a range of settings.

In order to manage life sentence prisoners the following, underlying principles are followed:

- they are treated as a group whose special needs are recognized within the prison, though not necessarily by separation or special privileges.
- they have a planned and structured career through the prison system and where appropriate, progress to conditions of lower security.
- their allocation to prison establishments is managed centrally.

A typical life sentence prisoner will go through a number of stages of the sentence prior to release on licence. There is no fixed time scale:

- Local Prison—whilst on remand, and perhaps for a short period after sentencing.
- Lifer Main Centre—usually one of three prisons at present for men—Wormwood Scrubs, Wakefield and Gartree. It is unusual for a prisoner to spend less than three years in a Main Centre.
- Category B training, or dispersal prison.
- Category C prison.
- Category D (open) prison.
- Pre-release employment scheme—usually hostel based, in the community.

Against such a background lifers in prison seek to live their lives. Ten years ago I met Julian in a lifer main centre. In his early twenties, he had recently been given his 'tariff—the minimum time recommended by the trial judge, and confirmed by the Home Secretary, following an opinion on it from the Lord Chief Justice. It does not guarantee a release date, and where release does take place, it is usually three years after the expiry of the tariff. For Julian, the tariff was twenty-five years, and the impact on him was devastating. 'I know the wrong I've done, I acknowledge my guilt, but twenty-eight years in places like this doesn't bear thinking about. I don't know if I can hack it.'

It is hard to imagine how he felt, his guilt and remorse compounded by the length of his tariff, more than the number of years he had already lived. In his despair he could only see darkness, and had he the courage, he said, 'I'd have killed myself, but that would be too easy. I have to be punished for what I've done.'

During the years which followed Julian and I spent much time together, discussing his offence, what had led to it, why he might have done it, for even he seemed to lack an explanation. He worked in the Braille Unit, spending three years obtaining his City and Guilds qualification, as he prepared Braille material for school textbooks, the TV Times, and anything else that was needed by those without sight. Such was his dedication to helping such people that he eventually purchased his own Braille machine in order to work in his cell at night. Every few months, with the permission of the governor, I transported the tins of food he had purchased in the prison canteen, and stored under his bed, to a night-shelter for the homeless in Leeds.

Two small gestures, as he saw them, of giving something back to the community he had deprived of a life. Symbolic gifts of restitution and reconciliation to a community disinclined to accept, inclined only to retribution. Yet, those acts contained within them, as restitution does, some element of healing, unlike retribution, which only inflames hatred. Julian, however, refused any part in his healing, determined to punish himself. Belief in God could not be translated into personal reconciliation, forgiveness, love. There was to be no 'cheap grace' for him, and I sat with him, empty-handed, my Christian 'tool-kit' for repair and restoration, useless.

Julian is still in a maximum-security gaol, his progress through the stages outlined above is slow. But with at least another eighteen years to do, there seems little urgency. I think he presents little risk to the public, but there are those I have met who have been inside for over thirty years who, I believe, are not ready for release, and may never reach that point.

Shane is one. Despite his years in 'the system' he seems to be stuck in a mental time-warp upon which behaviour programmes for offenders have had little impact. He shows no sign of increased self-understanding, much anger, and an inability to cope with any form of rejection. He seems as likely to reoffend now as ten, or twenty years ago. For some, life may have to mean life.

The Lord is merciful and gracious,
  slow to anger and abounding in steadfast love.
He will not always accuse,
  nor will he keep his anger for ever.
He does not deal with us according to our sins,
  nor repay us for our iniquities.

(Psalm 103: 8–10)

God of life
you are merciful and gracious;
slow to anger,
and of great goodness.
You offer us the possibility
and the potential
to be more than we are,
to respond to your
promise of love and
forgiveness.
Touch us with your grace
that in our disillusion
we may hold to you.

We hold before you
those who are 'doing life',
that in them your presence
may be acknowledged.
We commend to your care
those who feel the stigma
of being 'lifers', aware that
they will always be 'on licence'
and rarely free to be
the person they would wish.

As Jesus was stigmatized,
but never deserted, so we
ask that you be with those
for whom life is diminishing.
As Jesus was transformed
by your power into new life,
so may the gift of life
be available to all your people.

CALENDARS, DIARIES, AND THE WORD ▣

'**G**IVE us one of them diaries, mate', is a frequent request around the landings of the prison and not just at the start of the year, but throughout. So too is the demand for calendars. Most of those who ask would never be seen in the chapel where diaries and calendars are always available. And yet for many, the diaries which the chaplaincy makes available courtesy of the Lord's Day Observance Society, and the calendars, from the Trinitarian Bible Society, may be the only Christian reading material they will ever see, let alone request. For some, the material with its Scripture text for each day of the year is the means by which they begin to reflect on the Christian message, and there are stories told of lives being transformed through its use.

Whilst some people simply want something for nothing, and others a diary 'that's just the right size for my pocket', there are those who have said that the words in the diaries or on the calendars have caused them to think again about some of the things Christianity is saying. A few have said they have reconsidered the direction of their lives. Terry spoke for some. 'Prison really tries to destroy your spirit. It's a bad place to be, man. There's not much good here, yet the diaries help you cope, like. Some of it's a bit soft, but some has meaning.' In this way the seed may be sown.

It was in 1978 that the Reverend Noel Proctor, then chaplain of HM Prison Dartmoor asked for a few diaries to distribute. The Lord's Day Observance Society responded by sending him 150. Within two years the society distributed 24,500 to 93 prisons. In 1997, a figure of 90,000, to 165 prisons within England, Wales, Scotland, and Ireland will have been reached.

The availability of calendars in many languages is also of great help and can bring joy to some of the foreign nationals detained in prisons in this country.

He sustains all things by his powerful word.   (Hebrews 1: 3*b*)

I planted, Apollos watered, but God gave the growth.   (1 Corinthians 3: 6)

———

Blessed Lord,
who caused all holy Scriptures
to be written for our learning:
help us so to hear them,
to read, learn, and inwardly digest them
that, through patience, and the comfort
of your holy word,
we may embrace and for ever hold fast
the hope of everlasting life,
which you have given us in our Saviour Jesus Christ.

(*The Alternative Service Book 1980*, Collect for Advent 2)

FIRST TIME . . . ONLY TIME? ▨

A *YOUNG man in his mid-twenties, a professional person who had been born and educated in one of the former Eastern European countries, his English was fluent and articulate. It was his only experience of prison, arising from a situation which reflected a complicated dispute concerning his ethnic origin. A situation, however, with which I could identify, given my own roots. I felt I could echo 'there, but for the grace of God, go I'. Such situations do exist and this young man had been in one of them, and was paying the price.*

A regular member of a congregation in the Orthodox tradition, he adapted with surprising ease to the informal and non-liturgical acts of worship which I led in the chapel adjacent to the wing where he was held. Services were attended by some adult prisoners, and some young offenders. I was able to get him a copy of the Bible in his native language, thanks to one of the Bible Societies. He was grateful and our discussions continued over the weeks he was in prison. He was interested to hear about this book and he offered to write something about the questions which arose from the incident and his subsequent imprisonment. He wrote:

If we are prepared to accept, for a moment, that the course of our lives are predetermined, then we can give consideration to the expression 'it was meant to happen,' as a way of explaining an obviously injust term of imprisonment in one's life. It is right to say that throughout the centuries, mankind evolved accustomed to the existence of an all-powerful God to whom we attribute the control of our lives. Therefore, it is to God that people rightly turn in their darkest moments, echoing invariable questions, 'Why me?', 'What have I done to deserve this?'

There are no direct answers to this kind of question and consequently people are often left in a state of self-analysis, particularly where someone is innocent. There is no satisfactory answer in prison and so this state exists on release.

In fact, this is the state I am in at the moment, as I approach the end of my sentence. Frustrating as it is, I haven't found a compelling reason why God has given me such an experience, such a terrible trial. I've been through so much over the past year.

Returning to the initial issue, if it was really meant to happen, then I'm left wondering why I was given this imprisonment. I'm a professionally educated and disciplined man, a worthy contributor to society. What was this unfortunate experience supposed to have taught me?

Imprisonment, without doubt, can be one of the worst living nightmares and had it not been for my self-discipline, my ability to accept limitations, this whole experience would have become an even greater nightmare. This is how I am left contemplating. What am I supposed to have learnt from this trial? It was not until the final part of my sentence that I understood I was not to learn something, but it was to *show* me something. Imprisonment has shown me a side of human nature that otherwise would have been impossible to know in depth, first hand. I have also come to realize the importance of my girl-friend in my life, and the depth of our relationship has grown. But even so, on the eve of my release I am still wondering, why such a terrible price to pay for revealing something that could have been made obvious in some other, less frustrating way?

And it is in considering these questions that I accept that God works in mysterious ways, and his ways are indeed, at times, incomprehensible. But in all, I tend to believe that every difficult and arduous trial given by God is for the better, that adversity may be in fact a blessing in disguise, and that God walks with us through life's storms, and that great gain can come through great loss.

In the end, it is the apostle Peter that clearly expresses my hope:

Now who will harm you if you are eager to do what is good? But even if you do suffer for doing what is right, you are blessed. Do not fear what they fear, and do not be intimidated . . . For it is better to suffer for doing good, if suffering should be God's will, than to suffer for doing evil.   (1 Peter 3: 13, 14, 17)

Accept suffering and be redeemed by it.   (Fyodor Dostoevsky)

> Lord God,
> in our quest for answers
> we often reveal more questions.
> Help us live with uncertainty
> in an uncertain world.
> Enable us to discover
> that which is good,
> even in our suffering.
> Surround us with the mystery
> and joy of your love,
> that at the end
> all things may be understood
> and all may be well.

NAMES ▩

THE vans, the 'sweat-boxes', waiting to transport their charges to courts throughout the region, were lined up in the prison yard. Winter grime had made it easy for the graffiti writers: 'monster transport' was written in large letters down one side, 'criminal carrier' one of the more repeatable adornments on the back.

A recent proposal in England calls for the newspapers to 'name and shame' 15–17-year-olds who presently cannot be named, by law. John Braithwaite, an Australian criminologist, is one of the foremost proponents of this approach, which he calls 'reintegrative shaming'. He contends that punishment must shame the offender, and in so doing bring home the reality of the offence to that person. He acknowledges that to succeed such shaming must be reintegrative or it may become stigmatization and thus, counter-productive.

Braithwaite argues that it is possible to express disapproval through shaming within a relationship which is based on respect for the offender. It is shaming which focuses on the sin and not the sinner.

The danger is stigmatization, and the frequent use of names such as 'monster', 'pervert', 'evil', and 'beast', by the media helps to create outcasts of some offenders. A few years ago, a 14-year-old delinquent who found safe refuge from the police in a ventilation system on a housing estate was soon being called 'Ratboy'. It was left to his mother to affirm who he was as a person when she declared, 'He's not a rat. He's my son.'

And within the prison the most obvious 'outcasts' are those people on Rule 43, particularly the sex offenders, the 'nonces', as they are named by others.

Such name-calling, or shaming can certainly affect those on the receiving end and the stigma attached can be incredibly hard for some to bear. In an environment where relationships are tenuous at best, there is often little attention paid to the whole person and to their potential to be more than just 'names'.

As one-time Archbishop of Canterbury, William Temple, reminded us, 'The prisoner is never only a criminal and nothing else . . . it is good to think more of what the man may become than of what he is . . . to treat the character as what it *may* be is to treat it as what in actuality it *is*, for it *is* chiefly potentiality' ('Ethics of Punishment', 1930).

The soldiers also mocked him, coming up and offering him sour wine, and saying, 'If you are the King of the Jews, save yourself!' There was also an inscription over him, 'This is the King of the Jews.' (Luke 23: 36–8)

Lord Jesus
you were named, and mocked.
Mary's son, transforming
the stigma of death
with dignity and self-respect
rooted in faith.
As you called for forgiveness
for those who mocked you,
grant to us that spirit.
As we were named in baptism
so may we enter into life
and achieve our potential in you.

SEGREGATION ▨

I N the Segregation Unit, where a chaplain visits every day, and is required by the Prison Act to see all Church of England prisoners, and anyone else who asks, the staff asked: 'Do you want to see Smith?'. 'Yes,' I replied, 'anyone and everyone.' 'He's a bit of a mess,' was the response. As I was led to the 'strip cell', my heart rate increased and my anxiety rose. The 'strip cell' is used as little as possible and it has a concrete bed, just inches off the floor, and a concrete stump with a wooden top, which is a seat. There is no window and nothing on which a prisoner might do himself an injury. The door opens outward, and as it did I saw the blood stains on the walls, and the floor. Dried now, they seemed like enormous tears, the visible signs of this man's internal anguish.

I entered and crouched down on the floor beside the slightly raised concrete/wooden bed, displaying in this gesture my own vulner-ability. He was writing, hesitantly and with a fraughtness I had often seen in him on the main wing. Quietly, I said 'Hello'. 'The voices have left me,' he said, 'but now I don't know how to cope with my thoughts.' He continued writing, a list of thirty-five causes of personal concern he could express at that moment.

The upper part of his body was naked, the canvas (untearable) sheet covering his lower body. The bloodstained bandages covered both wrists. The signs of other, self-inflicted injuries continued to his elbows.

Two officers remained close by, sensitive to my need to commu-nicate with this man by myself, but near enough to be aware of any change in him, or me. My safety was their concern.

He talked rapidly and in myriad directions. It was clear that we could only begin to engage when he returned to the Main Wing. I encouraged him to do so, and days later we met again and talked.

I left the cell, stepping over a grating which covers the drainage system which allows such cells to be hosed-out, power-cleaned, washing away the visible signs of inward pain.

> Father,
> in the depths of anguish
> you are there.
> In the brokenness of our lives,
> you are there.
> In the torment we inflict on
> each other, you are there.
> No situation is beyond your presence.
> In our gestures, in our words,
> may we recognize you.
> In symbolic and simple action—find you.

WORSHIP ▦

'I T'S a short step between heaven and hell,' said one prisoner in a group discussion. We had been talking about the place of the chapel in the lives of those who attended, and this comment referred to the fact that access to the chapel, in this prison, is directly from the twos landing,* on a wing with about 200 hundred people. The contrast between the noise, clamour, and occasional violence of one, with the peace, relative comfort, and prayerfulness of the other, is just metres.

The chapel is used for a number of different activities, all of them in keeping with its primary purpose, that of providing a place for worship. It is here that the worshipping community of the prison gathers week by week as part of that offering made by the whole Church.

The worship style is varied, depending on whether it is led by an Anglican, Methodist, Roman Catholic, or Baptist member of the Christian Ministry Team. Always, it seeks to 'connect' to the experience of those present in some way, especially through the intercessions.

In worship we try to give 'worth' to God, and to each other. Sometimes it happens more easily than others, and when it does, those moments of 'transcendence', when the ordinary and the mundane are transformed, become moments to be treasured, and in which God seems so active.

Clifford, shortly before his release, provided such a moment. He was an able reader of lessons and I asked him if he would lead the intercessions this particular Sunday. He did so, with background music provided by a cassette of hymns played on classical guitar. The track was 'Be still for the presence of the Lord'. Apart from this, and the sound of Clifford's voice, not a sound could be heard. Even those from without the chapel could not impinge on the created silence. When he had finished, people simply sat, in the presence of God.

Clifford, as a prisoner, spoke from the same 'place' as other members of the congregation that morning, and he started by affirming the worth of each before God. With his permission, I reproduce the 'core' of his prayers:

Father;
Help us to face and accept the reality of our present situations, whether we are here for days, for months, or even longer.

Help us to admit past mistakes and also the consequences of our actions, the damage to others.

Help us to take that further step—to find true repentance in our hearts, and help us to show this clearly and honestly: to ourselves, to the world, and, above all, to you.

Help us to achieve that honesty in ourselves which will give us the courage to take a new path—for the sake of our loved ones and for the sake of our relationship with you.

Help us within our present enclosed world to temper resentment and aggression and to show understanding and fellowship towards both our fellow inmates and towards staff.

Help us with the world outside—to show family and friends that we need their love, loyalty and support; that we receive this thankfully—and that we respond.

Help us to open ourselves fully to you, to accept that we need above all else your love and support—and to have faith that this will always be given—that the burden of being made in your image will be eased by that faith and by our knowledge of you.

May our present situation be used by you to sanctify us.

After the silence that followed these prayers, we started to prepare for communion. Despite the frustrations of making relevant worship in this place, where else could I have the privilege of standing with people who would be amongst those Christ invites to the banquet? That morning, the body and blood of Christ was shared with sex offenders, robbers, fraudsters, drug addicts, alcoholics, and a murderer. In these people I meet Christ and share with him, and them, in the joyful task of the proclamation of God's love. During communion the organist played the tune St Botolph, and the words of Brian Wren's hymn, 'Christ Making Friends', came to mind:

> I come with Christians far and near
> to find, as all are fed,
> man's true community of love
> in Christ's communion bread †

A moment in worship can provide a glimpse into the mystery of salvation.

NOTES

* The twos landing refers to the second floor level, which is to be found in many prisons. Landings are known as, the ones (ground floor), the twos, the threes, and the fours.

† I come with joy to meet my Lord', Brian A. Wren, *More Hymns for Today*, no. 140.

YOUNG OFFENDERS ▩

I N 1997 the average number of sentenced male young offenders was 7,560,
a 16 per cent increase on 1996.*
    *They are a group of people who are often more demanding and difficult
than any other in the prison system. They are frequently frustrating, verbally
aggressive, and requiring particular skills of ministry. Fiona Eltringham was
one of the first women priests within the Church of England and was, at the
time of writing, chaplain to Castington Young Offender Institution in
Northumberland. She is now chaplain of Durham prison.*
    *Fiona, in the piece which follows, gives some insight into the essential gift
of faithfulness, so crucial in prison ministry:*

Michael was a bigot, or so he would have us believe. To him, Irish,
Roman Catholic, male (him) equalled good. English, Protestant,
female (me) equalled bad. It was in the light of this apparent bigotry
that we built up a pretty solid relationship over a period of two years.
He attended most of the chapel activities so we saw each other at least
twice a week and cheerfully hurled abuse at each other.

But Michael was an intelligent young man and the façade of bigotry
he had built up hid a lot of pain. He had been orphaned as a child and
he had been convicted of a particularly nasty crime that he had to keep
secret from other prisoners if he were to survive the system. I think
there was only one occasion, when in a private interview for the
purpose of a parole report, a little of the façade slipped and a hurt,
sensitive young man was revealed.

In many ways I did nothing for Michael apart from always being
there, listening if he had something to complain about, and giving back
as good as I got when the banter was flying.

After he was released, I had a letter from him thanking me for my
kindness. Kindness . . . ? I was only ever rude to him. In the envelope

was a prayer. Apparently Michael's mother used to give a copy of the prayer to anyone she knew who was in trouble. When she died a friend carried the habit on for her and so Michael himself eventually received a copy when he came into prison. The letter told me he thought his mother and her friend would approve of him giving his own copy to me.

It is a gift I treasure. I trust God goes with Michael and I continue to pray for him regularly.

So let us not grow weary in doing what is right, for we will reap at harvest time, if we do not give up. (Galatians 6: 9)

Fiona's prayer:

> **Heavenly Father,**
> **Help us to love others in the same constant way you love us,**
> **not seeking great results but remaining faithful.**
> **Thank you that we only have to sow the seed and that the**
> **growing is up to you.**

Note: Surveys of the prison population have revealed that of those prisoners under 21 years of age;
- 65 per cent had significant school truancy records.
- 75 per cent had been suspended or expelled from school.
- 25 per cent had experienced literacy problems.
- 20 per cent continued to have literacy problems.
- 8 per cent had attended a school for children with learning disabilities.
- 70 per cent had left school without any qualification.
- 33 per cent had been in care, 38 per cent as a result of their criminal activity.

The level of mental illness, especially that determined as 'serious' amongst young offenders is far higher than in the wider population. Some 53 per cent of the young male remand population has a psychiatric diagnosis, as compared with 33 per cent of the sentenced population. The most common disorders in both groups were substance abuse and personality disorders. The level of psychoses in the young remand population is four times higher than that in the community.

NOTE
* The peak offending age for male offenders is 18 years of age.

JUVENILES ▨

I saw him in one of the long, characterless, corridors of the Young Offender Wing. Looking lost and forlorn, Timmy seemed too young to be in such an austere, and intimidating place. At 15 years of age it was not his first time in trouble, but it was the first time he had been remanded in custody. One of about 1,889 boys aged 15 or 16 remanded to prison in 1995, his vulnerability was apparent. Of the 1,889, over half did not receive a custodial sentence when they were dealt with by the court. In one Young Offender Institution, 250 young men aged 16–17 are held on remand, 50 more are aged 15. Between mid-1996 and mid-1997 the sentenced male juvenile population rose by 28 per cent, from 1,260 to 1,620.

In mid-1997, 74 girls aged 15–17 years were in prison custody, a trebling of the numbers since 1992.

Timmy, not even old enough legally to leave school, found his new surroundings intimidating and difficult to cope with as he waited for trial. We sat in his cell as he recounted his story with such speed that the sentences seemed to be continuous, reflecting his nervousness and anxiety. His parents had divorced and his mother had formed another relationship. Unable to form a positive relationship with her new partner, Timmy spent increasing time on the streets, getting involved with joy-riding when he was 11 years old.

Repeated minor offending caused further alienation from his family and from his school environment. Experimentation with drugs led to reliance on them and within a short time of his fourteenth birthday he was heavily involved in theft in order to pay for his 'habit'. Eventually, when repeated cautions from the police had failed, and when he had stolen from his mother, Timmy was arrested and remanded in custody. Now, he waited, in an environment not likely to do him any good, but very likely to cause him harm, mental, physical, emotional.

The Criminal Justice Act of 1991 introduced provisions which should have brought an end to all remands of juveniles into prison custody. In 1997, it has yet to happen. The legislation relies on a sufficient number of secure accommodation places being available before it can be implemented. In April 1996 there were only 274 secure places, a fall on the 1993 figure of 295.

Whilst Timmy, and others like him, are held in prison accommodation, they may face emotional trauma, physical or emotional abuse, with consequent psychological damage. Such a scenario does not bode well for the future of such young people.

In 1989 the then Chief Inspector of Prisons in England and Wales, Judge Stephen Tumim, noted: 'In many ways these youngsters have less in common with young men in their late teens than is generally realised. They are often despised by the elder group, resented for their childishness and become victims of intimidation.' He went on to say that the number of juveniles kept within prisons was 'the most disturbing aspect' to come out of his inspections. The current Chief Inspector, Sir David Ramsbotham, in evidence to the influential Home Affairs Committee of the House of Commons, said the same.

> Gracious God,
> 'slow to anger and of great goodness',
> we express our frustrations
> at the inadequacies of 'systems'
> which fail to reflect the needs
> of your people.
> In a damaging world,
> unstable and confusing,
> we pray for the young
> held in prison,
> that damage may be limited;
> that meaning may be kindled,
> and self-worth fostered;
> that failure may be seen
> as a chance for a new start.

CHRISTMAS ▓

C HRISTMAS Eve, and the tree was being removed from the Wing where it had been placed just a few days before. Its fallen needles exposing its barrenness. Its removal, a symbol of the marginalization of the Christmas story which seemed to reflect my mood, itself a mirror image of an institution ill at ease with the 'festive season'. Exposing too the difficulty I find in connecting the joy and hope of that story with the lives of those 'inside'.

Later, as members of the Christian Ministry Team delivered a hand-addressed Christmas card to over 700 prisoners, a few were thrown back at us. In such a gesture the 'rejection' seemed curiously personal, a rejection of 'self' as much as of God.

Christmas is a difficult time for many in prison, for their families, and the sombre mood seems in stark contrast to the world outside. A colleague in another prison wrote to me, a note which arrived on that same Christmas Eve: 'It (the previous Christmas) was depressing. It was as if the season of goodwill had passed us by. Some men were in tears while others made the best of it by writing letters home to mother, wife or girl-friend—or boyfriend. Others had no one to write home to so they hid themselves away knowing that this most painful time would soon be over. Indeed, on Christmas Day last year I found one guy wrapped up tight in a blanket—like an Egyptian mummy—on the bed in his cell. He told me that he was in hiding and was not prepared to come out until it was all over. This was his first Christmas inside and during the previous nine months his wife had left him, his father had died, as had his grandmother.'

At home, I read in the *Church Times*, some words by the Primus of the Scottish Episcopal Church, the Most Reverend Richard Holloway. He said there were times when 'hope is low, and I am visited by a clear sense that there is no meaning and no beyond'. I fully concurred with him. But he went on to speak of the mystery of faith, and of our need 'to look at him whose birth we celebrate'.

The next day, Christmas morning, I had led one service, and now started another in the Prison Health Centre chapel. The congregation preferred not to sing carols. 'Too painful', said one, and the others agreed. A Rastafarian, who later spoke in the service about his experience of discrimination and oppression, requested the hymn 'Hail to the Lord's Anointed'. A powerful hymn about the mystery of the Incarnation, its words provided the means of connecting the divine story of the birth of Jesus, with those in chapel.

> He comes to break oppression,
> To set the captives free,
>
> His name shall stand for ever,
> His changeless name of Love.
>
> (James Montgomery, 1771–1854)

> May he defend the cause of the poor of the people,
>   give deliverance to the needy.
> For he delivers the needy when they call,
>   the poor and those who have no helper.
>
> (Psalm 72: 4, 12)

Lord, before you
we express our doubt,
and our faith;
our anxiety
and our certainty;
our quest for meaning
threatening to overwhelm
our sense of your presence.
In your Son
we acknowledge
the mystery of faith,
the encouragement of hope,
and the joy of his birth
as 'God with us'.

EASTER ▒

T HE *Easter acclamation rang through the chapel. 'Alleluia! Christ is risen.' And the response, from the prison congregation came back to me. 'He is risen indeed. Alleluia!'*
On this morning the sun shone through the chapel windows, its force obliterating the thick iron bars, thoughtfully designed in the shape of the Cross, to proclaim the freedom of the faith—or the constraints of Christianity? It hardly mattered. Bars in prison are not a thing for comment.

I faced a group of men who had decided to come to chapel that Easter morn. As with congregations 'outside', their motives were mixed. When it came to the sermon I used the following piece, written by a prisoner then serving time for robbery. It struck a 'ripple of responsiveness', and a few people said afterwards, 'I could have written those words—that's how it is for me. I ain't religious, but it said a bit about where I'm at.'

Gerry, who wrote it, called it 'Thought at Easter'. I have added a Bible reference and a prayer.

I'm not the kind of person who is ever likely to go to church, except of course for the obligatory weddings and funerals. I've never been much of a Christian. I'm not a Hindu, a Buddhist, a Muslim, or a Jew.

Religion tends to bore me. After all, religion is only something man invented to make him feel good—isn't it?

It's about that time of year that Woolworth's are going crazy trying to sell Easter eggs. The kids are happy, two weeks off school, an abundance of chocolate, all in all Easter's generally a nice time.

This Easter I'm in prison. This Easter I haven't seen a single chocolate egg. I regard the Bank Holidays with indifference. Two more slow days in prison, that's all. This year, for the first time ever I've thought about the significance of Easter. We all know the story, Jesus died on a Cross, then he came back, and Matthew, Mark, Luke,

John and the rest of the boys decided they'd better tell the world about it.

We can't actually deny the truth in it. It's all in the Dead Sea scrolls, and other old manuscripts that prove it. But what's so special about this Jesus? In 1,993 years' time I expect Mother Teresa will have achieved cult status. People like Terry Waite will go down in history as good examples, for all men and women to follow. So why is Jesus so special, why not Joan of Arc, or a host of other people who died for a cause? Tonight I read all about Easter in the Bible. The whole story, from the donkeys and the palm leaves to the Resurrection.

When you really do think about it, it's easy to see what Christians all get so excited about. Whether Jesus was the Son of God or not isn't a question that I can personally answer. What I can say for sure is that he was flesh and blood like me. Jesus was a mortal man. He knew what was coming, and understandably he was sad and frightened at the prospect of his death. He actually prayed to God the night before he died. He did not want to die, yet he left it in God's hands. He trusted God.

Jesus knew that his friend Peter was going to sell him down the river. He knew that on the day of his death, three times Peter would deny him before the cock crowed. But he accepted this, he never judged Peter, or anyone. On the day he died people had a chance to save Jesus from the Cross, but they all stood and allowed the crucifixion to carry on. Jesus was taunted and humiliated. He had a crown of thorns wedged on to his head, cutting deeply into his scalp. Then he was nailed to a Cross. Imagine the pain, huge nails driven through his hands and feet. The Cross was stood up and it fell into place in a hole that had been dug for it.

Now, Jesus felt the pain you or I would feel if we were on the Cross. At one point he actually uttered, 'O Lord, why have you forsaken me?' Jesus was a man who had suffered incredible cruelty and humiliation, and now, he was left hanging in the sun to die. Then, as he was on the Cross, he forgave everyone. He forgave Peter for selling out, he forgave the actual soldiers who had drove the nails through his flesh. In all that pain, all he could feel was compassion for all the people who had taken his life. He died asking God to forgive humanity its sins.

When I stop to think about that, it blows me away. I'm in prison for breaking the laws of the land. Fine, I can accept that. But sometimes it saddens me that the world will never really forgive me. I'll always be a robber in the eyes of many people. But when I think of Jesus up on the Cross, I feel humbled. All of a sudden, the few years I have to spend here don't seem to matter that much. As I said earlier, I've never been religious, but I do want to be forgiven by someone. I'm sorry for the wrongs I've done. The judge doesn't know how I feel, the police really don't care, and the victims of my crime probably find little peace of mind in the fact that I'm sorry for what I've done.

But Jesus, up there on that Cross, forgave people like me. He doesn't judge me, he doesn't hate me. He knows my wrongs, yet he still loves me. This is the first Easter I'll be spending in gaol. The first of a few. But it's also the first Easter that I've actually realized what it's all about.

_____

'And we indeed have been condemned justly, for we are getting what we deserve for our deeds, but this man has done nothing wrong.' Then he said, 'Jesus, remember me when you come into your kingdom.' He replied, 'Truly I tell you, today you will be with me in Paradise.' (Luke 23: 41–3)

_____

> Lord, the thief responded
> to the presence of your Son.
> Help us to know his presence with us
> that we may be transformed.
>
> Jesus, remember us when you come into your kingdom.
>
> As the thief acknowledged his need,
> help us to be honest about ours.
> And in repentance help us to
> confess our sin.
>
> Jesus, remember us when you come into your kingdom.

In the glorious light of the Resurrection
enable us to amend our lives
and to live as your people,
assured of your love and forgiveness.

Jesus, remember us when you come into your kingdom.

II
SITUATIONS IN PRISON LIFE

BETRAYAL ▨

H IS was a new face at worship. A Rule 43 inmate, segregated from other prisoners (except for other Rule 43 men) at all times, except in this chapel. In some prisons segregation is constantly maintained, even in chapel. In a few instances separate services are held for the Rule 43 men. We were few in number that morning and I took the decision to move the focus of the service from the main altar to an improvised one using the coffee table, with easy chairs in the round.

It was a Eucharist and as usual in that type of prison I tried to explain what was happening as we came to each part. We sat in a circle and he sat near to me. In such a situation I take some responsibility for the safety of such men, despite the presence of two officers. They too sat within the circle. Sitting in the round means no one is separate, but part of the body. Within it, all are accepted in a way that is not possible anywhere else in the prison.

As it happened the reading took the form of meditation; I asked people to try and enter into the reading, to use their imagination to become one of the characters; to enter into the Scripture to discover insight for themselves, to absorb the scene, to try and be there; to let the story generate personal ideas.

The silence was acute as I improvised the reading around Matthew's account of the betrayal of Jesus. Afterwards, we spoke. He was not sure why he had come. The previous night he had felt he must come to chapel the next day. He thought the feeling would pass, but it did not and in the morning he asked to attend chapel. He was glad he had taken the step.

'I have been betrayed, and have betrayed,' he said. 'It was incredible how relevant that Bible story was. I never thought of Jesus having been betrayed, but he was, and I know what if feels like. I see him in a new light—perhaps he was like me.' He had connected the divine story with his own, and in the process had begun to deal with an aspect of betrayal. Jesus, a powerful figure in his imagination, somewhat feared and distrusted, became a brother in the experience of betrayal. Unlike this man, Jesus never betrayed.

See, my betrayer is at hand.   (Matthew 26: 46b)

Lord Jesus Christ
in your betrayal
you knew pain.
In our betrayal of others
we ignore the pain
we cause.
Help us attend to your story
that, through it we may
connect it with our own.
That through it we may begin
the process of healing
that leads to reconciliation.

CHILDREN ❈

GEOFF, a cleaner on the threes landing called me over to his cell door. With a smile on his face, he said, 'Bill, I saw the kids last week.' His joy was evident. 'The Social Worker brought them up, not together, the 5-year-old one day, and the 7-year-old the next.'

I was touched by his joy, saddened at the depth of his anguish. He had endured uncertainty in their months of separation and he frequently said, 'Will I ever be allowed to see them, just once?' Now, he had. 'It was great to see them,' he said. 'And I've written letters for them to read when they're 18 explaining everything.'

At this point I found it hard to hold back my tears, even though I lived with the knowledge of his offence. Geoff continued his story, finishing off by telling me how the children had each thrown their arms around him at the conclusion of their visit, and said 'I love you Daddy.' Almost as an afterthought, he added, 'Those words will keep me going for years.' Many years, for he is serving a life sentence.

Geoff's memory of those two visits will connect him with his past and will help to sustain him in his future. This connection between past events and our present touches upon a mystery which is deeply rooted in biblical tradition.

The people of Israel, in remembering God's great acts of love and kindness seem, somehow, to enter into the acts themselves. The act of 'remembrance' is then more than just looking back at past events. It becomes a way of bringing those events into the present—to be celebrated and affirmed. Central to the biblical tradition is that God's love for his people should always be remembered and acknowledged in the present, in us now.

Geoff's former wife had agreed to this one visit. Despite the legal rights of fathers to see their children, many do not, believing that a pursuit through the courts is not in the interest of the child.

———

But Jesus said, 'Let the little children come to me, and do not stop them; for it is to such as these that the kingdom of heaven belongs.'   (Matthew 19: 14)

———

**Loving Father
in your Son
we see your love for all people.
We pray for the children
of those in prison,
parted from a parent.
Help us to understand
their needs and anxieties
as they try to make sense
of separation and pain.
Surround them with your love.**

**Lord, your Son responded
to the needs of children,
and through them proclaimed
something of your Kingdom.
We hold before you
imprisoned parents.
Relieve the pain of
separation which is theirs,
the joy which they
have missed and
the sadness they cannot share.**

HIV / AIDS ▨

T HEOLOGY has to be applied. It has little value if it is abstract, pure, and with no connection to the reality of people's lives. Most people 'do' theology in some form, each day. For many people, the development of the AIDS virus raises profound theological questions, and anyone ministering to people with the virus has to develop a theology which takes account of those who suffer with the consequences of infection, and who may themselves have worked out a theology to give meaning to their predicament.

In May 1996 there were eighty prisoners in England and Wales known to be HIV positive, or to have AIDS.

Peter Westwood was Anglican Chaplain of Brixton Prison when the predictions of the number of people likely to suffer from AIDS was at 'epidemic' proportions. Brixton Prison set aside a special unit to cope with the predicted numbers, and many other units were planned in prisons throughout the country. The chaplaincy, ahead of many agencies, produced HIV and AIDS, A Manual for Chaplains, providing much useful information. The scale of the predicted problem did not become manifest. A number of chaplains, including Peter Westwood, now retired, were involved in ministering to those who were, and are, infected. Peter tells something of his story, undergirded with a deep compassion. I have added a prayer to the Collect which he chose.

We now live with AIDS, uncomfortable and with alarm, but we live with it. It was not so easy fifteen years ago.

In prison, before programmes to provide education and awareness were in place, I found myself ministering in situations where police officers, wearing special protective clothing, were bringing people who were suspected and confirmed AIDS sufferers into the prison. Staff and prisoners were apprehensive and afraid. It became even worse when the medical view became known that those who were HIV positive, but well, did not need special accommodation or care, and therefore would live in normal prison cells, amongst other prisoners, and staff.

When identified, those people were put in the worst cells, discriminated against by staff and prisoners. Fear of possible infection was real, and suspicion only very slowly changed to understanding. Even in those early days when we all feared the worst, chaplains were able to hold out the hand of acceptance and make life a little more bearable for those involved. I remember spending a lot of time listening to the fears of prisoners, and officers, and trying to help towards a rational understanding of the disease, and trying to promote good practice in caring for those affected.

In a small number of cases I had been amongst those who accompanied sufferers on their final journey. All of those people were allowed to die outside prison.

Prisons are, by their nature, painful places, places where people suffer many small deaths as they go through their sentence. However, the facing of actual physical death in prison is unbearable for everyone. As a young chaplain, an old prisoner, who had done a lot of his 'bird', told me that he did not want to die in prison, and that is every prisoner's prayer. Yet, we are faced not just with the death of the old, but the young; someone who is looking at life, and hoping for a better future; to getting out of prison, living long enough for a cure to be found.

Every life is unique, and every death. But these young men had to face the anger, frustration, and sometimes the guilt and loneliness of death in prison. As a pastor, the tears and the rage I felt seemed to be overpowering. As also, the times of quiet, resentful acceptance, which were deep, and became too much, too painful to bear. Then we cry, 'To whom may we turn for help, but to thee, O Lord'. The prison ministry, if it does make any Christian sense, is a ministry of the Cross. It is where the incarnation is probing into the weakness and folly of humanity. We, of course, cannot bear much suffering. Too often it may seem to help if we can blame others. Some say it is 'God's vengeance', that God punishes homosexuals and drug addicts by giving them AIDS. But when we do that we are simply seeking the comfort of a small, convenient God. That is not the word of the incarnate Jesus Christ, the Good Shepherd, the friend of sinners, the one who mixed with the outcasts and the lepers. The problem raised by suffering is not solved by the incarnation, but it is changed by involvement, and by love.

Our grace and strength is the reflected radiance of Jesus Christ, and particularly Christ on the Cross.

With Jesus we might say 'My God, my God, why have you forsaken me?'   (Psalm 22: 1).

But we also pray, with hope:

> **Almighty Father,**
> **look with mercy on this your family**
> **for which our Lord Jesus Christ**
> > **was content to be betrayed**
> > **and given up into the hands of wicked men**
> > **and to suffer death upon the cross;**
> **who is alive and glorified**
> > **with you and the Holy Spirit,**
> **one God, now and for ever.**
>
> (*The Alternative Service Book 1990,* Collect for
> Good Friday)

> **God of suffering and compassion**
> **hear our prayer**
> **on behalf of all who suffer**
> **with HIV or AIDS;**
> **for all who fear the possibility**
> **of developing the virus.**
>
> **God of peace, be generous**
> **in your gift of peace.**

God of wisdom, be in the
choices people make, and
in their consequences.

God of courage,
give to all who suffer disease
the courage manifest
in your Son.

God of love
we pray for those
whose loved ones are affected by HIV or AIDS.
Inspire them with hope,
and the joy of unending love,
which has the power to change all things.

FORGIVENESS ▧

J OHN was 23. Three years earlier he had been diagnosed as being HIV positive. The woman he lived with had been a prostitute, an intravenous drug-user, but she had never told him.

Returning home one day he was told she was in a local hospital. When he got there and explained who he was, he was asked, 'Do you know she has Aids?' Devastated by this revelation he watched, and waited for her to die, within a few short months. She was 26. Carrying with him a profound anxiety about his own health, he was eventually persuaded to go for a test. It confirmed what he felt he already knew. He was HIV positive. She had infected him.

Three years have passed and his immune system functions at about half the 'normal' level. Since returning to prison he has returned to faith; a faith which came about through the care shown him by a Christian family at the end of his previous sentence. Nothing dramatic had taken place for him, no 'Damascus road' experience; just the conscious building on the care shown to him, and attention to the suffering of Christ. 'In his suffering', he told me, 'I see something of my own'. John went on to explain how he felt about the forgiveness which Christ expressed towards those who caused his suffering. As a result of his faith, he said he had forgiven the woman who had infected him. He had watched her die, been with her, and when she had said 'sorry', he had forgiven her. Three years on that sense of forgiveness was uppermost in his mind.

As so often in prison, I was left with a question, to which I could not provide an answer. A question arising from his capacity to forgive, borne out of love. I wondered if I could ever have a similar capacity?

'Father, forgive them; for they do not know not what they are doing.'   (Luke 23: 34)

———————

God of forgiveness,
help us forgive.
God of forgiveness,
help us know forgiveness.
God of forgiveness,
help us know
peace in forgiveness.
God of forgiveness,
help us know
love in forgiveness.
God of forgiveness,
help us know you
in forgiveness.

Lord, it is difficult to forgive,
to know what it really means
to offer it, to accept it.
Yet you never give up on us
and always accept us.

LISTENING ▣

TREVOR was typical of many people in prison. He wanted someone to listen to him, to take him seriously, to acknowledge who he was, and to accept him 'warts and all'.

He took every opportunity to speak to me, rarely giving me much opportunity to respond to his endless flow of words. It took much attentiveness to discern what might have been behind some of what he said; time and patience to help him express some of the thoughts which lay deeply buried within his mind.

So many of those in prison have such harrowing stories to tell that the responsibilities of those involved in active listening are great. At times it requires enormous effort, perseverance, and patience. Sometimes I think we listen with only one ear—only half-listen, too often presuming that we know what the other person is likely to say. And the assumption that we have to say something in response is an affliction which needs to be resisted (particularly by the clergy).

All too often, Trevor left what he really wanted to say to the time when our conversations were coming to a close. The temptation to ignore what is being said at that moment is easy, particularly if the pressure on time is great, as so often it is.

Dietrich Bonhoeffer, in his book, *Life Together* (SCM, 1975), is scathing about the ability of some Christians to enter fully into the 'Ministry of Listening', saying they are too busy talking when they should be listening. He goes on to say, 'One who cannot listen long and patiently will presently be talking beside the point and be never really speaking to others, albeit he be not conscious of it. Anyone who thinks that his time is too valuable to spend keeping quiet will eventually have no time for God and his brother, but only for himself and his own follies.'

For those who minister in prison, where there are so many

demands, so much noise, so many things to be attended to, this is a salutary reminder, and in the Bible the verb 'listen' is used more frequently than the verb 'speak'.

Bonhoeffer concludes his section on listening with the words, 'We should listen with the ears of God that we may speak the Word of God.'

If one gives answer before hearing,
it is folly and shame.

(Proverbs 18: 13)

Lord God
you are more willing to listen
than we are to hear.

As we seek to listen
to those with whom we speak,
help us to acknowledge the
privilege and service
to which you have called us;
to respond to that trust.

In the clamour of our lives
we confess our fear of silence.
In our need to speak
we fail to hear the thoughts
of others; fail to hear your
presence.

Give us the gift of the
'ears of God, that we may
speak the Word of God'.

RELATIONSHIPS ▨

EVERY new prisoner, on remand, convicted or sentenced, is required, under the Prison Act 1952, to be seen by the chaplain, or as happens in practice now, a member of the chaplaincy team. During the interview it is rare for a prisoner to claim to have no family or friends, no significant relationship.

Yet frequently, the relationships which do exist, within or without the prison, are damaged, tenuous, unpredictable, and there is a high rate of breakup between prisoners and their partners, separation from their children and home community. There is bullying, assaults on staff and on other prisoners, self-harm, and suicide. Prisoners are frequently far from their home area, making visits by relatives and friends very difficult for some. Increased numbers of people in prison can also affect the quality of relationships as staff have to deal with more people, with less time available to care for those in need. It may also mean some prisoners being moved from one part of the country to another, often at short notice, and with little regard for the impact on their relationships.

An additional, and complicating factor relates to the number of people held on remand who should be in alternative custody, for example, in the care of the National Health Service, or a Secure Unit, because of their mental state. Being remanded in prison can lead to increased despair and anxiety for those people, for a worsening of their condition, and for those staff who care for them, a feeling that they are ill-equipped to provide appropriate support. ·

At the very heart of Christianity lies an understanding of the character of God which is based on the concept of relationships. It is exemplified in Andrei Rublev's Icon, *The Hospitality of Abraham*, in which three people, three angels, sit around a table. Representing the Trinity, they are three persons in relationship, Father, Son, and Holy

Spirit. The deep significance of this view of the Holy Trinity is well expressed in a Report by the British Council of Churches, *The Forgotten Trinity*. 'If God is essentially relational, then all being shares in relation. There is . . . a relational content built into the notion of being. To be is to exist in relation to other beings.'

Relationships between prisoners and their families, between prisoners and staff, prisoners and prisoners, staff and staff, are a crucial element in creating peaceful, co-operative, and positive regimes in prison. In the Scottish Prison Service, for example, where the importance of relationships has been given greater acknowledgement, policies have been formulated which reflect the importance of the relational dimension. So, there is a commitment to try and place every prisoner within thirty miles of his/her home. In contrast, a 1994 survey in England and Wales found that prisoners' relatives had to travel on average sixty-two miles to visit them. In Young Offender Institutions the figures rose to over 100 miles. Increasing pressure on available accommodation in many prisons means this situation is likely to continue for the foreseeable future.

Then the Lord God said, 'It is not good that the man should be alone; I will make him a helper as his partner.'   (Genesis 2: 18)

> **God of love,**
> **in the Trinity**
> **we see relationships**
> **as they might be.**
> **Individuals, but**
> **sharing in common.**
> **Separate, but united.**

Forgive our lack
of love and respect
for each other,
our ability to disregard
our commonality in
pursuit of our individuality.
Help us affirm our relationships,
that, together we may be nurtured.

NOTE

Of those remanded in custody 20 per cent are acquitted. Another 36 per cent receive a non-custodial sentence—sometimes because their time in prison on remand is taken into account, but sometimes because their offence is not deemed to justify a custodial sentence at all. Such figures reflect a widespread injustice to many remand prisoners, and their families.

REMEMBRANCE ▨

THE daily 'reception' list of those who had arrived in the prison the previous evening was on my desk. I saw Ben's name, location, age, racial origin, number, and religion. Jewish. In conversation he explained his background, but said he did not want to see the Orthodox Rabbi. I undertook to try and find a Rabbi from the Progressive, or Liberal tradition.

In the mean time I gave him a copy of the Jewish Daily Prayer Book, the Haftorahs and Pentateuch, and the Tanakh. Over the following weeks he spoke with me frequently. Never at great length but always in depth. He asked to become the Chapel Orderly when the post became vacant. Essentially a cleaning job, it should never be restricted to Christians.

Ben was seen by a Progressive Rabbi. In our talks and in discussion groups his interest in his faith tradition began to develop. He began to be put in touch with his memories of childhood and Jewishness.

The memories which we have, within or without prison, play a central and crucial role in our sense of being, in our joy and in our pain. The feelings which we possess of grief and satisfaction do not depend only on the events, but on our memory of those events.

Ben began to explore those memories, to 'remember' his past, his tradition. As he did so, he began to connect his own story to that of his Jewish forebears. In remembering, he began to explore the tension between his past and his future and through it he began to rediscover his identity and find a new meaning for his life. We need to pay attention to the memories which are presented to us, for they have the power to change hearts. We sometimes have the privilege of helping people explore their memories, sometimes the joy of seeing them healed.

'Then when you call upon me and come and pray to me, I will hear you. When you search for me, you will find me; if you seek me with all your heart, I will let you find me.'   (Jeremiah 29: 12–13)

'Remember the days of old, consider the years long past.'
(Deuteronomy 32: 7)

> God of Israel
> teach us to remember
> our past with gratitude.
> Enable us to remember
> your goodness and your love,
> that we may be your people now.
> We give you thanks
> for the gift of memory,
> for its part in shaping us
> and making us who we are.

VULNERABILITY ▨

A COLLEAGUE said to me, 'What can I do when I'm in the Segregation Unit? I feel helpless, at a loss to know what to offer.' I responded by acknowledging my own difficulty in such situations, but believed in the concept of what sometimes seems to be 'useless presence', a way of being with people, not of doing. Later, Cathy wrote of one such experience, and each of us has added a prayer:

I sat very still and listened as the story unfolded. It began slowly, very slowly at first. It took time to tell because it had never dared to be told before. Well, how do you begin to share the pain and misery of a life systematically destroyed? Where do you start when all your childhood memories run red with blood, black with fear, and blue with coldness and brutality, the agony as vivid today as it was all those years ago? Who do you trust with that deep, open wound that is your life, and what will be the price you pay, if, having finally trusted someone, they let you down?

Suppressing an urge to move, I remained still, waited as the tears were wept, and the rage was expressed; staying as open and vulnerable as I could, risking as much as the story-teller. As calmness descended and the tears began to dry Frazer asked, 'How did you do that? How did you help me to cry? How was that possible?'

How? It's simple, and difficult. There is only one real way into the pain of another. It involves risk to self, no doubt, but that is the price which has to be paid. Vulnerability is the key that opens the door of vulnerability. Nothing less will do. It is all that can be offered that is of any value, that is authentic. Vulnerability alone speaks to vulnerability. As it is offered, so is it recognized and welcomed, like a friend, like a soul-mate.

In the harsh world of prison there is little room for any show of what might be seen as weakness. So any vulnerability is screened from prying eyes. The need, however, to express the pain, the anger, the fear, and the frustration remains. The chaplain has no need to collude with the macho image of the prison system, for the model for all Christian ministry is that of Christ himself, the epitome of vulnerability, hanging high on a Cross, arms open wide. His refusal to defend his dignity, to protect his name, to save his life, resulted in his death, but that ultimate expression of humanity has touched the lives of millions for nearly two thousand years.

Is it too much to ask to be listened to by a fellow human being, to be treated with respect, to be given the opportunity to tell it how it was, without fear of the broken, shattered dreams being trampled into the ground all over again? To be vulnerable is to be human, but to share that, is to be Christ-like.

———————

A broken and contrite heart, O God, you will not despise.

(Psalm 51: 17)

———————

> Loving God,
> we come to you
> just as we are,
> vulnerable and afraid.
> We reach out to you
> in trust and faith,
> praying that in you
> we will find peace,
> acceptance and encouragement,
> through Jesus the Lord.

Lord, in your Son
we see the cost of being vulnerable
to the expectations of others,
of being open to their pain
and vulnerability.
As we encounter
those whose lives are broken,
help us confront our brokenness
to commend it to your
healing and transforming power.

LOST INSIDE ◼

T HE HOWARD LEAGUE *is one of a number of penal reform groups seeking to encourage debate about all matters relevant to crime in the community and criminal justice policy. In October 1997 it published its findings into the imprisonment of teenage girls. Fran Russell is Assistant Director of the Howard League. In this edited version of an article which first appeared in the Howard League's magazine,* Criminal Justice, *she describes some of the findings. The concluding prayer was written by Brian Dodsworth, a former prison chaplain.*

Charlie is 17. Her mother is an alcoholic and Charlie has never known her father. Charlie's mother often used to hit both Charlie and her brother on a regular basis. She also burnt Charlie and slashed her neck with a knife. At four years old, Charlie was taken into local authority care for the first time. She has been back and forth between various children's homes ever since. At 13 Charlie was raped. Three boys dragged her into a park. She reported the rape to the police but, as with the majority of allegations of rape, 'nothing happened'. She said her mother only seemed concerned she had torn her uniform.

At the children's home she claims a staff member tried to sexually assault her. She 'kicked-up' and was originally charged with criminal damage but the charge was dropped when the full story came out. Charlie attempted suicide in the children's home and said she probably would have tried again in prison had a friend from home not been there as well.

Charlie had a baby girl three months before she was sentenced. The baby is now being looked after by her 17-year-old boyfriend, who is the child's father, and his mother.

Charlie was an extreme case but not untypical of the other sixty girls interviewed by the Howard League's inquiry into the use of prison custody for girls and all nine prisons holding teenage girls were visited. The inquiry was set up because of the increasing number of girls being sent to prison. Between 1992 and 1996 the rate more than trebled from 79 throughout 1992 to 214 in 1996. In addition, 224 girls aged 17 were held on remand.

The girls interviewed were all between 15 and 17. All were damaged and vulnerable young women.

- 40 per cent had been in care.
- 65 per cent had experienced broken families.
- 57 per cent were excluded from school, or were long-term non-attendees.
- 41 per cent admitted to drug or alcohol abuse.

Large numbers had suffered some form of sexual, physical or emotional abuse, had poor relationships with their parent, if indeed their parents were around at all. Many had abused drugs and alcohol, had chronically low self-esteem, and many had turned to prostitution at some time to get the money to survive and to pay for drugs. Many had been brutalized by the adults around them and the system had failed to protect them.

Contrary to general impressions, most had not been convicted of serious offences nor were they persistent offenders. 42 per cent of the girls interviewed had either no previous conviction or had previously received only a caution or conditional discharge, suggesting that the courts were not using prison as a last resort as required under the Criminal Justice Act 1991. Nearly half of those who had committed violent offences against the person had either themselves been the victims of violence or they had witnessed violence in the home, usually against their mother or siblings and by either their father or their stepfather. A third had been given short sentences of six and a half months or less indicating that their offences did not make them a danger to the public. Nearly all of the girls interviewed said they had never come across self-mutilation before they came to prison, yet 22 per cent of them admitted they had cut themselves or attempted suicide.

In its report *Lost Inside: The Imprisonment of Teenage Girls*, the inquiry concluded that the prison system is ill-equipped in dealing with such a young age-group. Since most of the girls would not have got a custodial sentence had they been boys or convicted four years previously it recommended the government should actively promote the use of non-custodial sentences to reduce the numbers being given custodial sentences. For those children who genuinely require a secure environment it recommended they be held in child-centred institutions such as local authority secure accommodation units.

———————

Who will separate us from the love of Christ?   (Romans 8: 35)

———————

The light of God is round us;
The love of God embraces us;
The power of God keeps us safe;
The Spirit of God watches over us.
Wherever we are, God is there.

NOTE

In a separate report, *Young Prisoners*, published just a few weeks later, the Chief Inspector of Prisons, Sir David Ramsbotham said, 'The Prison Service should relinquish responsibility for all children under the age of 18.'

SELF-HARM ▩

Ian had lacerations from his wrist to his elbow, on each arm. When I saw him he had just cut both his cheeks. This latest attempt at self-harm was just one of over two thousand such incidents recorded in prisons in England and Wales in one year.

Studies have shown that of those who have self-harmed in this way some 10–14 per cent later die at their own hands—a potential 200–80 people. The chance of suicide is 100 times greater in such people than in the general population. Many of those who self-harm whilst imprisoned have already done so before they enter prison.

Some people have seen such incidents of self-harm as being an attempt at manipulation. It is more likely to be because the person is trying to communicate a problem which is beyond their control at that time. Some despair of what they perceive as an intolerable position which crucially highlights their lack of self-esteem, their limited control over events, and their inability to convey to others their deep distress. Some describe the feeling of intense relief which they experience once they have committed the act. It is thought-provoking, and disturbing, to consider that the letting of one's 'life-blood' may be the only way of finding relief, or drawing attention to a real problem.

As I sat with Ian, listening intently to all he told me I was aware of my inability to carry such a load. He was the second person to speak to me in such a way within an hour. It was a Sunday. I had already taken two services and it was only just mid-day.

What could I offer to this man? How could I help him? How could I respond to his needs?

The reading at one of the services had been from James, 'be quick to listen, slow to speak . . .' (1: 19) Was that enough, I wondered?

Frank Lake, one of the founders of the clinical theology movement, quotes the novelist Taylor Caldwell (*The Man Who Listens*): 'Man's real need, his most terrible need, is for someone to listen to him, not as a "patient" but as a human soul.' We could replace 'patient' with 'prisoner'. (Frank Lake, *Clinical Theology*, abr. Martin Yeomans (DLT, 1986).)

Ian had a learning disability, and had been fostered from the age of two. He was now approaching his twentieth birthday, and lived in a group home, under the policy of 'Care in the Community'. He was desperate, frustrated, angry with himself, and finding it hard to articulate his thoughts. I listened, finding it equally hard. Despite hearing it all from others many times before, it still pains me anew when I am faced with people like Ian; people who have never had any real chance, who have known little love, received little care; whose lack of self-esteem, self-worth, and self-understanding cry out through their words and actions.

'Big boys don't cry,' it is said. Ian did. And I, inwardly.

Taylor Caldwell's words filled my mind and I fought to concentrate on Ian's words, constantly 'sifting' them to try and understand what he was saying, to patch together a mosaic of sadness, to respond positively, but realistically.

———

You must understand this, my beloved: let everyone be quick to listen, slow to speak, slow to anger.   (James 1: 19)

———

Lord God
in their trauma
they scar themselves.
In doing so
they scar your image;
for we are created
in like form.
Created for life
they see only the negative,
the pain from
which they have come
and to which, so often,
they return.

Help us break the
cycle of destructiveness,
to give worth to those who
feel worthless,
control to those
without control,
hope to those
without hope,
that as with Christ
you may heal the scars
which afflict us all.

THOUGHTS OF SUICIDE ▨

FTER the morning service I deliberately sat next to one of the 'new faces' over coffee. At that time we had three services each Sunday, in three chapels located in different parts of the prison. Had all three congregations been together they would have made up one good-sized group. As it was, there were ten men at this communion service and I was able to give Alan some time. He had not been to church for many years and certainly not in the three montths he had so far been in prison. 'I'm not very religious,' he said 'I don't go to church very often.' Not an unusual line for ministers to hear, either in prison, or outside.

As we talked he began to reveal a little more about himself. I already knew he was a Rule 43 prisoner, segregated because of the nature of his alleged offence. Not that I was aware of the nature of his alleged crime, but I knew he came from the wing which housed such men. I also knew he was on remand. Prison seems to make some prisoners get to the heart of what they want to say very quickly, and Alan was soon telling me of a religious experience which he had in his cell.

As soon as such conversations start to go in this sort of direction my instinct is to be cautious. On this occasion I was intrigued by what I heard.

Alan recounted some of his feelings during his first few days in the prison some twelve weeks before. He had never been inside and had not expected he would be. In his cell he experienced powerful and recurring urges to commit suicide over a number of days. He spoke of these feelings to no one. One night he decided he had had enough, he was going to kill himself. Some memory from his childhood made him reach for the Gideon Bible.* Randomly he opened it and read the first words he saw on the page;

> The snares of death encompassed me;
>> the pangs of Sheol laid hold on me;
>> I suffered distress and anguish.
> Then I called on the name of the Lord:
>> 'O Lord, I pray, save my life!'
> Gracious is the Lord, and righteous;
>> our God is merciful.
> The Lord protects the simple;
>> when I was brought low, he saved me.

(Psalm 116: 3–6)

At the conclusion of verse 6 he read no further. Nor did he try to commit suicide. The thoughts remained with him for sometime, but knew he could not go through with the action. He attributed his change of mind to God speaking through the words of the Psalm. Now, weeks later, he was ready to encounter God in worship, to speak about what he felt to be God's action in his life.

Subsequently, Alan was convicted of his offence. Many months later he is still convinced about God's part in his being alive.

> **Faithful God**
> **we give you thanks that**
> **you rescue us from our faithlessness.**
> **Help us to hear your voice**
> **in scripture and the experience of those we meet.**
> **We give you thanks for**
> **the word which changes lives,**
> **for the word which affirms**
> **and gives meaning.**
> **Enable us to respond**
> **to your word as you**
> **respond to our prayers.**

NOTE

*The Gideons supply thousands of Bibles and New Testament and Psalms to prisons. For more about their work, see the Chapter, 'The Word across the Prison World'.

SUICIDE ▦

URING 1996, there were 64 self-inflicted deaths in prisons in England and Wales, almost one every five days. Of these, 36 were on remand, 26 deaths were amongst prisoners aged 25 and under, and 19 of the 26 were on remand, with six being under 21 years of age. Of the self-inflicted deaths 14 involved prisoners aged below 21 years. Sixteen of the deaths were amongst prisoners serving four years or more, or on life sentences. Their average age was 33. Two of the 64 deaths were women. Set against an average total prison population for the period of some 55,200, the figures show a higher rate than that found in the wider community, reflecting the significant proportion of men and women entering the prison system who are known to be highly at risk.

More than one of those 'statistics' was known to me. Rati was 26 years of age and was born in Sri Lanka. Convicted and sentenced to three years, he had served two and had come to the end of his time in prison. Now, he was being detained pending the outcome of discussions with the Immigration Service, who had advised him of the likelihood of deportation. He spoke good English and on a few occasions he came to chapel, even though he was a Hindu. Whilst I was on leave, he took his own life.

Those of us who knew him, just a little, felt we had let him down, had not recognized his isolation and his deep fear of deportation. The sense of loss was acute amongst the landing-staff concerned, particularly the officer who had shared a 'good-night' with him as he locked Rati in his cell only to find he had taken his own life. Rank and position faded as staff shared a common sense of grief. No relatives could be traced, despite extensive efforts by many people.

With the help of some members of the small, local Hindu community I arranged for his cremation. With five members of that community I sat in the crematorium chapel and thought of our failure. Rati, surrounded by people, had died alone, 'a stranger in a foreign land'.

Despite the 'coherent multi-disciplinary strategy' employed by the Prison Service, despite the increase of male suicide in the wider community, despite the 'high risk' of many in prison, despite the success of the Prison Service reducing the numbers of those who had taken their own life, despite my knowledge that not all suicides are preventable, I felt I had let Rati down.

I was reminded of some words of John Donne, 'No man is an Island . . . any man's death diminishes me, because I am involved in mankind'. With others, I share deeply, and ashamedly, in that diminution.

<hr>

How could we sing the Lord's song in a foreign land?

(Psalm 137: 4)

<hr>

Lord of life,
look with mercy and compassion
on those, who, in despair
have taken their own lives.
In your love may they
find light, peace,
and life eternal.

<hr>

NOTE
See also Thoughts of Suicide, Samaritans and Listeners, Self-Harm.

SAMARITANS AND LISTENERS ▨

'I FEEL absolutely exhausted,' said Mark, 'Joe's been in with me all night. He talked and cried most of the time. But I think it's helped him, he seems a bit more settled now, and we got a bit of sleep, eventually.' Mark is a prisoner, so is Joe, and he had only been in the prison a few hours when it became clear he was having major difficulties in coming to terms with this, his first experience of being 'inside'. One of the prison officers had suggested he speak to Mark, a Listener, and had arranged for them to be 'two'ed up'—to share Mark's cell for the night, giving them an opportunity to continue their time together in a way impossible for a member of staff. As a prisoner, Mark knew something of what Joe was experiencing, and his willingness to be alongside him, to listen, to give him an insight into prisons, was just what Joe needed.

Listeners are prisoners who volunteer for this role, but are selected, trained, and supported by the Samaritan organization in the local area. Nearly a hundred prisons in England and Wales are running such schemes, and they have proved to be a valuable resource, amongst others, in helping prisoners who are anxious, in despair, or potentially suicidal. In addition, direct access to the Samaritans is possible through use of the telephone, and often by seeing local volunteers when they come into the prison for 'surgeries', or simply on request.

Whilst Listeners cannot receive the same level of training as Samaritans, they are trained in basic listening skills and suicide awareness. They also have regular access to their trainers, and to those Samaritans responsible for supporting them and helping them to work through any difficulties, or feelings which they might be experiencing.

The Samaritan movement, founded in 1953, usually works in prison through the multi-disciplinary Suicide Awareness Team, to offer confidential, emotional support to prisoners, and, where necessary, to staff. Listeners and Samaritans maintain the principle of confidentiality inside the prison, as outside, with two notable exceptions: where accepting a confidence would contravene the Prevention of Terrorism (Temporary Provisions) Act 1989, or where a prisoner is obviously in the process of taking his/her own life, or where it is believed this may already have happened.

There are many people like Joe, who need help with transitional experiences, and other significant events in their life. Increasingly, there are more people like Mark, more Listeners, and more Samaritans, in prison. Such a sharing of responsibility, between staff, Listeners, and outside agencies, for vulnerable individuals is a reflection of a relational approach to caring in a complex environment.

Which of these three, do you think, was a neighbour to the man who fell into the hands of the robbers? He said, 'The one who showed him mercy.' Jesus said to him, 'Go and do likewise.'   (Luke 10: 36–37)

God of mercy and compassion,
we commend to you the work of
Samaritans and Listeners;
foster their ability to show
mercy and to hear the stories
of those who are anxious,
depressed or suicidal,
to accept them, and in so doing
to help the healing of hearts and minds.
May their ministry reflect
your purposes.

INNOCENT ▦

ANDREW and I first met when he had been incarcerated for fourteen and a half years. Immensely shy, this large and amiable man made a deep initial impression on me, and on my Roman Catholic colleague. He had recounted his story to each of us and had given us permission to reflect together on his situation. He had spent a number of years in a special hospital, for the criminally insane, and had now returned to prison as new evidence about his case began to emerge.

Many protest they are innocent of the crime for which they have been imprisoned. A few have convinced me, usually after a long period of time has elapsed. Andrew was different. He seemed to exude innocence and my colleague and I quickly formed an opinion that he was one of the few. Yet, questions came to mind, how could an innocent person have spent fourteen and a half years in prison? Surely all the evidence had been unequivocal? And believing him, how could we protest our belief in his innocence?

Andrew talked quietly, but with frightening clarity of his conviction, of his initial rage, bewilderment, and indignation at losing his freedom for something he had not done. His continued denial of guilt had probably contributed to his still being in prison, for the system does not cope easily with such dissent. Over those long years he seemed to have turned his feelings inward, on himself, but his anxiety rarely surfaced. His presence disturbed us both, as we colluded in his continued imprisonment, helpless though we were to do otherwise.

Within eighteen months he was freed, declared to have been physically incapable of committing the crime for which he served sixteen years in prison.

On television, I watched this man take his first, faltering steps of freedom, and the tears welled up. There were to be more tears. Two years later, he died. His story of innocence, vindicated.

And in their mouth no lie was found; they are blameless.
(Revelation 14: 5)

Father God
whose innocent Son
suffered death on the Cross,
we pray for those
who are imprisoned
though they have done
no wrong.
Enable us to sit
where they sit;
to support their plea
and to help them rise
with Christ, in joyful hope.

'GHOSTING'—JUSTICE, OR INJUSTICE? 🈁

'**B**E careful of that one, Chaplain,' said the officer in the Segregation Unit. 'He's here on a lie-down—he's been no bother, yet, but he has been in other places.'

Ever mindful of such warnings, I approached Stan with care as he walked around the small exercise yard. A space not much bigger than that afforded to a 'big cat', and just as difficult to escape from. Having introduced myself I walked by his side. Despite the confines of such places there is theological significance in 'walking with', in a ministry of presence. The summer sun shone on the fraction of the exercise yard it was able to penetrate. Our conversation was not much more enlightened, at least initially.

Stan told me a little of his story. He had been in prison for just over ten years, for a crime, he claimed, he did not commit. A claim I hear frequently, it is occasionally true. 'What has brought you to this prison?' I asked. 'I've been ghosted, again,' he replied. 'Ghosted' is the term used by many within the prison system to describe the process which is officially known as the Continuous Assessment Scheme. Aimed at severely disruptive prisoners, it involves being moved every twenty-eight days, from one prison to another. At the time of writing, twenty-three prisoners are on the scheme. It is planned to open a special unit for such severely disruptive prisoners in early 1998. In it, they would receive the sort of care needed to try and break the cycle of disruption.

Stan had been in nine different prisons since the start of the year. As if reciting a Litany, he named each one for me, with acerbic comments where appropriate. As always when I hear the accounts of those who have been 'ghosted' I was indignant that we only ever seem able to treat the symptoms of disruptive behaviour, not the causes which such men carry deep within them.

Over the days which followed Stan told me much about himself, about the prison system on which he is an expert, and about the powerful, negative effects his 'continuous assessment' has on his family, his friends, and himself. Such prisoners are never told exactly when they will be moving and on more than one occasion Stan's visitors arrived at the prison where he was being held only to find he had been moved. Personal possessions are minimal because of the movement. Letters take weeks and even months to 'catch up' with the prisoner. The stress imposed by uncertainty and new surroundings is considerable.

The effects of such a scheme may simply exacerbate the difficulties which such men have, leading to escalating conflict, not resolution. Their 'reactions' are then seen as justification for maintaining them on the scheme. Labelled 'disruptive', they may live up to that designation.

An alternative to the use of such coercive power needs to be sought if justice is to be done. Lord Justice Woolf in his report on the Prison Disturbances of 1990 said this 'carousel' approach to dealing with the most difficult prisoners should not be endorsed. The problem is made worse by the fact that the twenty-eight day movement rule negates any one prison claiming 'ownership' of that prisoner, and his problems. Just occasionally, a prison receiving such a prisoner decides its investment should be more than temporary control and succeeds in breaking the cycle, and in restoring something of self-worth and hope within the individual.

The philosopher, John Locke, said that human beings are the property of God and using this concept as his base, he developed the doctrine of natural human rights. It is because we are God's 'property', God's people, that we have rights that should protect us from abuse or mistreatment by another, be it an individual or an institution. Justice is not always easy to define, but we might do well to think first about injustice.

Now, let the fear of the Lord be upon you; take care what you do, for there is no perversion of justice with the Lord our God . . .
(2 Chronicles 19: 7)

While they were talking and discussing, Jesus himself came near and went with them.   (Luke 24: 15)

God of justice
open our eyes
to the injustice we create
in pursuit of order.
Enable us to respect
the rights of your people,
to seek for their good.
To show them the
way of peace, which is yours.

We pray for prison staff
entrusted with the duty of care
for such people, who are not
always easy to deal with,
or easily liked.
May duty be tempered
with compassion.

PAEDOPHILES ▥

THE number of convicted sex offenders in prison is just over 4,000, with 424 having been convicted of gross indecency with a child.

The subject of paedophilia is highly emotive and confusion over definitions often exists. A paedophile is a man (very occasionally, a woman) with a fixed interest in pre-pubescent children. Contrary to some people's opinion, they are not 'monsters', not easily identifiable. If they were, they would not get close to children. But they are people who believe that children can give their consent to sexual activity, indeed some believe that the children with whom they are involved have, somehow, 'encouraged them'. They are capable of identifying, encouraging, and seducing a child, often rationalizing their thought process by convincing themselves that the child is enjoying what is happening. If they have been abused themselves as children (and not all who are abused become abusers) they may convince themselves that they enjoyed such activity and that they gave their consent, and that the child with whom they are involved thinks in the same way. They are often people who have been emotionally isolated and have difficulty in coping with emotional stress, of low self-esteem, and poor at appreciating how others might be feeling.

Whilst they cling to the sort of belief system that enables them to abuse, they find legitimation is given to their acts and with support groups in this country and abroad, with magazines endorsing such thought processes, some feel they have not done wrong.

One man I knew who had regular sexual intercourse with his young daughter justified his actions to me by saying, 'It was an act of love, and my wife encouraged it to happen'. Such distortion and minimization must be challenged and since 1992 treatment has been available to this type of offender imprisoned for more than two years. In the twelve months from April 1996 to March 1997, 663 prisoners completed sex offender treatment programmes. The programmes are based on a form of treatment called 'cognitive behavioural therapy', and are aimed at altering the way in which men think about the images which arouse them and lead to illegal sexual acts. The programmes also help offenders to gain some sort of understanding of the impact their offences have on their victims, as well as helping them acquire the skills which they need to help prevent them reoffending.

The success rate of such programmes is high, with evidence from Canada showing that over a ten-year period convictions for reoffending can be reduced significantly. In a current research project in south-east London, sixty-five offenders have, following a careful risk-assessment, entered into community-based programmes. Two years on from the start of that project none has reoffended.

Changed behaviour is possible for some, though how far it is 'control' rather than 'cure', is the subject of debate.

As from September 1997, the Sex Offenders Act came into force. It requires offenders who have committed sexual offences against children to inform the police of their address and if they move they have to give notice of the change. Any change of name must also be notified to the police. The length of time an individual will have to be registered will depend on the length of sentence, but anyone gaoled for thirty months or more will be on the register for the rest of his or her life.

> **Lord God**
> **we hold in your presence**
> **all who distort your image**
> **in their distortion of childhood.**

We hold in your presence
those whose lack of self-esteem
and understanding
drives them to violate
the bodies of children.
We hold in your presence
the brokenness and bitterness
of those whose innocence
has been destroyed.

We hold in your presence
those who seek to bring
healing and wholeness
in word and deed,
confident of a resurrection story.

SEX OFFENDERS AND RELIGION ▒

I VAN had been convicted of a serious sexual offence. He had also 'found religion' in a big way, shortly after his conviction. In a simple way, which brokered no discussion. What I was presented with was 'the new man', the 'old' had been discarded, along with his victim. The offence no longer mattered, that had been committed by the 'old' man, and this 'new creation in Christ' was somebody different.

Such a firm conviction, black and white, is common in some offenders, and in some sex offenders in particular. When it happens, and when the past is denied in this way, it is very difficult for chaplains, or any member of staff to break through the façade which hides the reality which is the person. The use of common religious language with chaplains, volunteers, and others, may be one way of eliciting sympathy and understanding without it being realized by those people.

Ivan had come from a deeply religious family and occasionally such families may distort religious teaching in order to instil a fear of human sexuality in their children. When he was offered the chance to attend the newly created Sex Offender Treatment programme, Ivan declined, saying, 'I don't need to do anything like that. I've found the answer to my problems. Jesus and the Bible meet all my needs. Jesus has taken care of my problem.'

A preoccupation with reading his Bible, preparing a prayer-letter to send to sympathetic people throughout the country, and responding to their encouragement, meant he was 'cocooned' in a religious world where being 'born again' meant an alternative reality.

Any of my attempts to help him face up to his situation were met by rejection, 'You're not even a Christian,' he would say, 'when were you born again?' Any reply was never accepted. On one occasion, when I refused one of his requests I was threatened physically. And when it was known that I was to leave that prison, his prayer-letter carried a request for people to pray for 'a real Christian chaplain, unlike the one we have now'.

Ivan's credibility amongst those who received his prayer-letter and who read his letters in many Christian publications was enormous. His accounts of his 'work for the Lord' in prison led many Christians to give thanks for his ministry.

Chaplains, volunteers, Christians in the wider community, are often seen by some sex offenders as offering acceptance and forgiveness at any price. But there is a price, and it may be high. All who minister in prison need to be aware of their potential to be 'abused', and must not collude with, distort, or minimize the offences of those with whom they work.

Chaplains have a unique role to play in contributing to the faith-understanding and world-view of prisoners, and they can contribute to the success or failure of those who see religion as a cover for the past. It demands rigour, self-understanding, and training.

Would not God discover this?
For he knows the secrets of the heart.

(Psalm 44: 21)

God of understanding
we distort our conception of you
if we offer 'cheap grace'.
Help us to provide support
with challenge,
hope with realism,
encouragement with insight,
integrity with compassion.

Almighty God
to whom all hearts are open,
all desires known,
and from whom no secrets are hidden:
cleanse the thoughts of our hearts
by the inspiration of your Holy Spirit,
that we may perfectly love you,
and worthily magnify your holy name;
through Jesus Christ our Lord.

(*The Alternative Service Book 1980,* Collect
for Purity, Rite A)

VULNERABLE PRISONERS— RULE 43 ▨

I'M rarely in the prison on a Saturday, carefully guarding the only day we have as a family. On this occasion I had made an exception, for an ecumenical group of church people coming in to learn about the context and practice of prison ministry.

As I sat in the office putting the final touches to what I was going to say, the phone rang. An articulate woman told me that her father, over 80 years of age, had been sentenced to four years the day before. He was, she said, 'in a terrible state', and had been told immediately that he would be going to a prison for convicted prisoners many miles from his home, despite there being one much nearer, and more convenient for visits and the maintenance of relationships. Having been given my name by her vicar, I was now trying to answer a huge number of questions, for her mother, and her father. Gradually, I tried to fit the pieces together, and when she told me her father's location within the prison, the situation became clearer.

Ernest was on 'D' Wing, the Vulnerable Prisoner Unit, the Rule 43 Wing, or, in the language of most other prisoners, the 'nonces' wing'. Not all of the thirty-three men held there are sex offenders, but the assumption is that they are. They are all there for their own protection, and have usually requested to be 'on the Rule'. Some have allegedly committed sex offences, or, been recently convicted of having done so; some have got themselves into debt with other prisoners, perhaps drug or gambling related, and, unable to pay, have sought refuge away from the other wings. Given that Ernest had only come into prison the previous evening, I could rule out his being in the latter group. I assured his daughter I would see him as soon as possible, and to find the answer to some of her questions.

As I arrived in the Unit, Ernest was being 'signed up' by a member of the Board of Visitors, who are required to visit all Rule 43 prisoners within their first seventy-two hours, and to make sure they want to be 'on the Rule'. He and I sat in the Library, observing the usual rules whereby I could be seen by an officer, but we could not be overheard in conversation. Such a rule, for the safety of staff, seemed unnecessary in this instance, but had to be obeyed. Within a very short time, Ernest had revealed much of himself, and without prompting, spoke of the reasons for his conviction whilst strongly protesting his innocence, and denying the offences.

Ernest spoke quietly, deliberately, with great clarity, and a sense of deep hurt at being in such a place for the first time, subjected as he had been the previous evening to taunts of 'beast', 'monster', 'nonce', 'child molester'. Unlike some on the wing, he had experienced only verbal abuse, not physical. He had not been spat at, had urine thrown at him, or poured under his door, had his food interfered with, or been hit. For even here there is a 'pecking' order which seeks to 'grade' offences and to make scapegoats of those considered by some prisoners to have done something more reprehensible than they themselves have done.

I was deeply touched by his story, and I tried as ever, not to judge, but to listen, and to try and help him in whatever way was appropriate. As with his daughter, he was deeply troubled by the prospect of being in a prison so far from home, though he knew that the commitment of his wife and daughter would ensure they visited. But he had discovered why he would not be nearer home. It had been explained to him just before my arrival. He had been convicted of sexual offences, and the prison to which he wanted to go would accept him on its sex-offender wing, but only if he acknowledged his guilt. He would not, and refused to compromise his integrity by saying he was guilty, even though it would have made his visits easier, and may even have helped him to be released a little earlier. As I left, he said, 'say a prayer with me Padre'.

Later, I was able to confirm with a staff member in the Observation, Classification, and Allocation group that his explanation was correct. I phoned his daughter. By midday on Monday he had gone, but not to the prison of his choice. A reminder, too, of the immediacy of ministry in such a place, of having to make instant relationships, which hopefully reflect something of God's love. Sometimes, there are no second chances.

Just a few weeks later, I spoke to another man, Kenneth. He was in the Health Centre, his face bandaged, his hands encased in protective plastic, hiding burns caused by boiling water being poured over him. His waist area was heavily bandaged, following many kicks. Kenneth had declined the opportunity to 'go on the numbers', to be a Rule 43 prisoner, and had remained on normal location for some weeks without anyone knowing the nature of his offence. With just ten days to go before his release, some of those on his landing discovered why he was inside. A distorted and perverted form of 'justice' had been enacted, harshly and with incredible speed. It had been well orchestrated and was over in minutes. In court he had pleaded his innocence. On the landing, he had no second chance. The 'scapegoating' of others is a common coping mechanism used by some prisoners to divert attention from themselves, to avoid the need for self-examination. It is a cowardly action, but it can exact a high cost, as Kenneth discovered.

Do not judge, so that you may not be judged.   (Matthew 7: 1)

See what love the Father has given us, that we should be called children of God; and that is what we are.   (1 John 3: 1)

Lord, your Son
reached out to the
scapegoats of his time,
and those on the margins;
we hold before you
all who are isolated
as vulnerable prisoners;
those who live with
mockery, insult, and alienation;
so often regarded as less than human.
As we affirm the worth
of all your children,
so help us to foster
self-worth, dignity, and respect
in those who are vulnerable.

We pray for the staff
who work in such units,
for the patience to care
for the impatient and demanding,
for their ability to see
beyond the offence,
to the person.

NOTE
About 2,000 men are held in Vulnerable Prisoner Units throughout the country.

PRISONERS IN A FOREIGN LAND ▨

AKBAR had come to chapel, he said, 'because it is a safe place'. His English was poor, but understandable, which was just as well as I spoke no Farsi. Detained under the Immigration Act as he was passing through Heathrow Airport *en route* to another country, he was now in prison. He had not committed a crime, but felt strongly that he was being punished as if he had done so. Having escaped from a country where he feared for his life because of his political views under an oppressive regime, his sense of oppression had not diminished as he now faced uncertainty about his future. A Muslim, with a deep sense of the presence of Allah, he felt the chapel offered him a sanctuary, a place where he could be at ease, find friendship and support.

I was able, through a local Roman Catholic Justice and Peace Group, to contact two people who spoke Farsi and to bring them into the prison to meet Akbar. With their help he was able to articulate some of his concerns, which he had been unable to put into English. I was then able to speak to his solicitor and to the Immigration Service and to get for him the information which he needed to know about the 'process' he was undergoing. Gradually, his fears seemed to subside to a manageable level, and as they did his sense of isolation also diminished. His concern for his wife, still in his home country, remained a pre-occupation. Eventually, word came from her and communication started.

Over the next few weeks I got to know Akbar well, and one morning I went to the 4's landing to see him in his cell. He had gone, without warning, transferred to one of the Detention Centres for people held under the Immigration Act. Some 860 asylum seekers are currently detained in the United Kingdom, belying an estimated 6,000–10,000 detained for varying periods throughout the course of a year. In

October 1996, there were 155 who had been detained for six months or more. Thirty-four had spent over a year in detention.

In September 1997, there were 5,223 foreign nationals in the English and Welsh penal system, reflecting an increasing trend throughout European countries. Many are on remand, some are convicted, and some are held under the Immigration Act. In the words of one press report about British prisoners in foreign gaols, but apt here, they are 'the marginalized in a world of the marginalized'.

As with British prisoners held in foreign gaols, of whom there are about 2,208, many, like Akbar, suffer from a lack of information about the criminal justice system within which they are being held, the culture of the country, or even the way the prison runs. Not surprisingly, many foreign prisoners have difficulty with written or spoken English, and access to interpreters may sometimes be difficult. Cultural understanding, and the needs of the individual may also be a source of difficulty, leading to misunderstanding and conflict. Relationships with family members may be difficult to sustain and breakdown of relationships is common. For those in this country facing deportation, and with family members here, there is the prospect of having to leave without loved ones, even children.

Such difficulties lead to a heightened sense of loneliness, mistrust, and fear, causing considerable anxiety.

Many weeks after Akbar was moved, I received a telephone call, 'Akbar's okay. He still doesn't know what's happening to him, but he's hopeful, trusting in Allah.' We heard no more.

Father of all
in your compassion
hear the prayers of those
who are marginalized
within prison life,
for those imprisoned
'in a foreign land';
isolated through culture,
religion or language.
Be present in their
loneliness and uncertainty,
that they may hold
to your presence and love.

III
REFLECTIVE THEMES

EVIL ▨

Q
UESTIONS *about evil are an inevitable aspect of every thinking*
person's life. In the prison context the questions arise frequently.
Some people find it tempting to give easy answers, from a
psychological or theological point of view. I do not believe there are
any such answers. In the piece that follows, Dr David Wilson, a former
prison governor, and a Christian, provides insight into some aspects of the
concept of Evil. David had a wide experience in the prison service, and he
bases some of his thoughts on his relationships with prisoners labelled 'Evil'. I
have added a biblical reference, and a prayer, with David's permission.

Apartment 213 contained seven skulls, and four heads, three in the standing
freezer, and one in a box on the bottom shelf of the refrigerator. In the freezer
compartment of the refrigerator there were assorted body parts. In a blue
fifty-seven gallon barrel there were headless torsos, hands and assorted limbs.
There were also more than a hundred photographs of people taken at various
stages of dismemberment, most so disgusting that even seasoned police
officials could not look at them without feeling faint.

Why do people do appalling things to each other? How do we explain
the wanton destruction of life? Should our search for explanations
begin with psychology, psychiatry, genetics, or a range of environmental and social factors? To many people such a search is merely an
elaborate charade, aimed at finding excuses to forgive those whom
only God can forgive. The Nazis who ran concentration camps, Pol
Pot in Cambodia, serial killers and rapists, the Moors Murderers and
others like them. For this group of people, the argument runs, who
inflict pain and suffering without apparent reason, we don't have to
look too far or too deeply for an explanation—they are Evil.

This seems to have been the view of a Milwaukee court, who, a few
years ago, sentenced Jeffrey Dahmer, the serial killer, and occupant of

Apartment 213 mentioned above, to fifteen consecutive life sentences for the murders of seventeen young men. Despite his own explanation of mental illness, like Peter Sutcliffe and Dennis Nilsen before him, the judicial process preferred to see him sane, ascribe responsibility for his crimes, and thus find him 'guilty'. The fact that Sutcliffe and Ian Brady, one of the Moors Murderers, are now diagnosed as paranoid schizophrenics does not seem to have affected the judicial judgements about them, and nor, would it seem, do many people care. The moral and legal problems associated with judging people who do appalling things to other human beings are presented as rather arcane philosophical musings, interesting and academic, but with little role to play in the pragmatic matter of protecting the public through incarceration. However, pragmatism often leads to corners being cut, and a shorthand being used which aims to label, rather than to understand. One such label is Evil.

What follows is not intended to be a definitive analysis of Evil. Rather it is a series of observations, and thoughts about how others have used this word, and in what circumstances they have applied it to people, or events. Thus, I move rapidly from individual examples of people who have been described as evil, to historical or contemporary movements or circumstances. Inevitably this results in a patchwork, or collage, as opposed to something seamless, and I am conscious that the use of the word, and its application differs dramatically in effect when applied to the Holocaust as, for example, when it is applied to someone who physically or sexually abuses a child. However, it is precisely because the label has been applied so randomly that such connections are interesting, if only to make us question the validity of the label itself, or broaden our understanding of Evil.

The word Evil is, of course, associated with our dualistic Christian notions of Heaven and Hell, God and the Devil, and for thousands of years many people have been prepared to explain the wickedness of others in theological terms. Evil in this context is an independent force, operating with a mind of its own, seeking out converts with similar zeal to the 'Powers of Good'. (We are all familiar with the phrase 'the devil has the best tunes', which implies something of the supposed glamour and magnetism of this 'dark side'). Yet in the course of my job, as when I have had to work with notorious murderers and serial killers, people who have already been labelled as Evil by those who have never met them, I have never once felt that this description, applied in this way, was accurate, meaningful, or important. Perhaps in the same way that hand-to-hand combat, where one's opponent or victim is seen, is usually less terrible and destructive than using weapons which kill over hundreds of miles, so closeness to people who do wicked things allows one to grasp a complexity which distance denies. For Evil is not something which is separate and dynamic in itself, but rather something which is part of us all.

Some might complain that whilst this is all good and well, it does little to explain destructive and wicked acts, and cruel and unthinking violence. If Evil is part of us all, why does this shadow manifest itself in only a few, and in what circumstances? Can it really be possible that the most mild-mannered amongst us, given the right mix of factors, could turn into a monster, bent on death and destruction? Serial killers themselves find the answer to this question bewildering.

As Dennis Nilsen put it, 'no one wants to believe ever that I am just an ordinary man come to an extraordinary and overwhelming conclusion'. The steps that led him to that conclusion have been followed meticulously by Brian Masters, from Nilsen's lonely, unloved childhood, through his eleven years in the Army Catering Corps (where he learned his butchering skills), to his brief spell as a policeman, and finally to his days in the Kentish Town Jobcentre, and his nights in various gay bars. Masters concludes that Nilsen killed for company, 'to have someone to talk to, someone to care for', and that Nilsen was 'not a stranger amongst us (but rather) an extreme instance of human possibility'. What is it that makes this possible?

As psychiatrist Anthony Storr has observed, human beings are very destructive towards each other. Here I would not wish to enter into the debates about the acceptable use of aggression, whether aggression is innate or learned behaviour, nor to deny that aggression can sometimes be a positive act. What interests me instead is at what point aggression becomes translated into destructive violence.

It has been calculated that between 1820 and 1945 59,000,000 people died in Europe as a result of war, murder, or other acts of violence, and in particular in Auschwitz alone, at the height of the Second World War, 6,000 Jews, Poles, Russians, gypsies, homosexuals, and others were exterminated each day. Closer to home the National Society for the Prevention of Cruelty to Children calculates that 200 children each year die in Britain at the hands of their parents, or step-parents, and Childline, established to deal with the overwhelming reality of child abuse, receives thousands of calls each year.

The growing awareness of those who work with sex offenders that there is a cycle of abuse, in which those who are abused as children may go on themselves to abuse when mature, suggests something of the enormous importance of childhood in the development of individual personality and behaviour. Childhood is for far too many a baptism of fire, burning psychological scars deep into the unconscious. I have already alluded to Nilsen's unhappy childhood growing up in Fraserburgh, and similarly Peter Sutcliffe, who nearly died at birth, was a sickly, sensitive boy, who was regularly bullied at school. Nilsen's and Sutcliffe's childhood experiences are not uncommon, and instances of the horrific treatment of children who, unlike them, never survive beyond infancy are numerous and disturbing. I hope that two examples will suffice.

Some years ago, the *Independent* newspaper reported the trial in Bristol of David Hammond, who killed his daughter by beating her with his fists, then a ruler, plastic tubing, and a kettle flex, before picking her up by the hair, and throwing her into the bath. In the same year Danny Palmer killed his seven-month-old stepson by beating him about the head with a rounders bat, causing extensive bleeding to the baby's eyes, and lacerations to his mouth. The post-mortem also revealed that both the baby's arms had been broken just above the wrist. Does all this put some perspective on the 'Moors Murderers', Ian Brady and Myra Hindley, who bizarrely taped the screams, and pleas of their young victims to 'mummy and daddy', a transcript of which controversially formed the conclusion of Gordon Burn's novel *Alma Cogan*?

Children, who by their very nature are helpless and dependent, are thus ironically also the centre of their household. The reality of their inability to fend for themselves automatically places total responsibility for their well-being onto others, establishing new domestic hierarchies, and priorities. Some insecure adults find this threatening to their self-esteem, or may feel themselves replaced in their partner's affections, and if they themselves have been badly treated or abused as children, or made to feel worthless, the recipe for disaster becomes all the more apparent. What this serves to underscore is the importance of adopting a positive, rather than a punitive approach to children, and providing the necessary support to those parents who require help, in the form of child benefit allowances, crèche facilities, and nursery care. The link between childhood experience and adult behaviour is complex, especially since many of the most disadvantaged, or abused children go on to make outstanding contributions to our society, never dreaming of treating their own offspring cruelly, but it is none the less surely true to argue that children who are loved, and cared for in a stable environment, are going to be themselves in a better position to love and care for others in the years to come.

It is worth while to reflect on the childhood and personality of Jeffrey Dahmer, especially given the seemingly similar patterns of development that we are now aware of between Dahmer and Dennis Nilsen. Dahmer was brought up in a middle-class household where his parents spent much of their time arguing. His childhood was characterized by isolation and neglect. He had no close friends, and gradually withdrew into a fantasy world of his own making. When he was 12 his parents divorced, and his mother left home with his younger brother David, leaving him to be looked after by his father. He eventually enrolled in Ohio State University, but dropped out after one semester, and thereafter enlisted in the Army. Colleagues from his Army days remember that he was a 'different man' when he had been drinking, and Dahmer drank constantly, which eventually led to his dismissal. From the Army he gained employment in the Ambrosia Chocolate Company, where he worked until his arrest, and spent his evenings in Milwaukee's gay bars.

There is much in all this which is common to Dennis Nilsen. Both drank to excess, had had careers in the Army, were homosexual and personable enough to 'pick up' their victims. Of greater interest was their similar childhood experiences, characterized by isolation and loneliness and being abandoned by those whom they loved. In Nilsen's case his beloved grandfather died, and in Dahmer's his parents' divorce resulted in his mother leaving home. Dahmer was later to claim that it was his dislike of being left alone that led him to kill his first victim, a hitch-hiker to whom he had offered a lift. Both used to take photographs of their victims, partly as a masturbatory device, keep body parts in their house, and would seem to have existed in a fantasy world, partly formed by alcohol abuse, in which power, control, and status denied to them in reality was theirs for the moment.

Depersonalizing as a means of subjugation or gaining acquiescence is a common device employed by 'total institutions'. On reception into prison, for example, the first thing that will happen to you is that your personal clothing will be taken from you, and you will be provided with a uniform. You will be asked to bathe, symbolically washing away the 'outside world', given a number, symbolic of the new 'inside world' you have joined, and informed of a set of rules which place you at the bottom of a hierarchy in which you have no control and little power. Individual personality becomes subsumed by a group identity, and a system of life is established dependent not upon personal preference, but on the needs of the organization. When the needs of the organization take priority over the needs of the individual, abuse is inevitable, allowing custodians to justify ill-treatment as a consequence of the need for 'efficiency', 'economy', or other similar rationalizations.

The examples above, of cruelty and destruction, come from deep within the imagination of Man. The ability to see others as less than human, to rank them according to perceived status, creed, sex, or colour, stems from a conscious capacity to analyse and think. The development of ideologies, the choosing of options or courses of action on the basis of that analysis, is the necessary prelude to violent behaviour. Imagination, Man's greatest asset, is also his Achilles' heel. To see another as evil requires an imaginative capacity not found in animals, and it is Man's capacity for abstract thought, his ability to give meaning and purpose to his life, incorporating the knowledge of his own ultimate death, which elevates him beyond the animal world. It is his discontent with the way the world is which gives him mastery of it, but that mastery has to be tempered by reason. But reason is often the first casualty when tempers fly, or tongues or fists are loosened by alcohol, or when one group or individual wants to feel more important or valued by asserting superiority over another. Of course imagination cannot be controlled, but it can be shaped and moulded given the proper circumstances.

Significantly, both Dennis Nilsen and Jeffrey Dahmer inhabited a fantasy world of their own making, and in another context sex therapists have drawn attention to the power of fantasy as a prelude to sexual assault. These fantasies invariably place the protagonist in a position of power and importance. Thus in this respect we could end cruelty and wickedness tomorrow by beginning to value all who live in our world, regardless of their size, their sex, their colour, their religion, or political affiliation. Undoubtedly this aspiration is a forlorn hope, but if we start by recognizing that no one is 'Evil', separately, totally, dynamically, and that instead the roots of wickedness are in us all, we may at least begin to grasp the way forward.

I consider that the sufferings of this present time are not worth comparing with the glory about to be revealed to us. For the creation waits with eager longing for the revealing of the children of God; for the creation was subjected to futility, not of its own will but by the will of the one who subjected it, in hope that the creation itself will be set free from its bondage to decay and will obtain the freedom of the glory of the children of God. We know that the whole creation has been groaning in labour pains until now; and not only the creation, but we ourselves, who have the first fruits of the Spirit, groan inwardly while we wait for adoption, the redemption of our bodies. For in hope we were saved. Now hope that is seen is not hope. For who hopes for what is seen? But if we hope for what we do not see, we wait for it with patience.   (Romans 8: 18–25)

Lord of all creation,
in acknowledgement of our
capacity for evil,
we are silent before you.

The silence of despair
can overwhelm us
as we reflect on our ability
to mar your image,
and to walk in the path of self-destruction.

Fill us with faithfulness,
with a 'groaning'
– a quiet cry—which
enables us to contemplate
in redemptive silence.

May we be filled with hope in Christ,
in the power of the Spirit,
and in the certainty of a vision
for your future glory.

NOTE

The inspiration for this prayer comes from some words of L. Gregory Jones, in his book *Embodying Forgiveness* (Wm. B. Ferdmans Publishing Co., Mich., 1995).

ANGER

ALBY *is 29 years of age, a life sentence prisoner. He has done ten years in prison for manslaughter and is currently on a course of therapy in Grendon Prison, a therapeutic community. Alby provides us with an insight into one who has perpetrated physical violence. It is easy to be outraged at such acts, difficult to begin to understand what may be behind them. Understanding will never of itself lead to solutions, but it does provide us with a glimpse of ourselves. Alby concludes his piece with a deeply personal prayer, to which I have added a more general one.*

Lord, I cried out to you last night. I said, 'God help me,' and I felt nothing. Maybe I didn't feel you with me when I prayed because I don't deserve you. I wanted to feel some spark within myself. I wanted to hear words like 'Yes, I love you.' I wanted to feel your arms around me. I felt nothing.

I cried last night in my cell, and I've never cried in my cell like that before. It's make or break time for me. I got through it before because I was stoned. Now that's not possible.

Lord, I'm not a monster. I'm a good man who did a very bad thing. **I know what I've done**. I stabbed a woman fifteen times, to death. I heard her pleas and I ignored them. I know that. That's here in my heart. **I know what I've done**. Sometimes I feel like writing to the Court of Appeal to say 'Can you give me another ten years on my sentence?'

I was up from twelve to four in the morning with suicide thoughts. I said I would kill myself at 29 because my mother was 29 when she killed herself. I thought, 'I'll give these people something to think about.' I can't, of course. I've got people who mean something to me, and I think if I kill myself I'd be a lost soul.

I'm sick to death of these cold callous people who pass judgement on me. I want to get hold of these people because (God forgive me) they are cruel. Now I've got two more years of having to say, 'I'm a sex offender. What objectives have you got for me?'

They don't know what life is like. They were just little talcum-powdered kids; then they went to college.* It's wrong to think like this. I don't really like myself seeing them as scum bags. But I've been raped in prison one hundred thousand times by their questions.

In 1989, if you'd let me out, you'd have had a serial killer. Now I don't want to hurt people. **I know what I've done**. I've left untold numbers of victims.

But I'm sick of it. There's a human being here.

O God, you know the frustrations I feel and the difficulties I go through as a human being. You know my heart and true desire. In the midst of all this, I pray.

> **Lord, your Son was not afraid**
> **to express his anger.**
> **Help us to voice ours,**
> **to own that which may**
> **provoke us to verbal**
> **or physical reaction.**
> **As we seek to understand**
> **the 'self', enable us to**
> **acknowledge what we are before you,**
> **in order that we might become what**
> **you would have us be.**

NOTE
*This is a reference to psychologists/therapists. See also, Wholeness and the Therapeutic Community.

REMORSE, OR REPENTANCE? ▨

'HE shows no remorse,' said the probation officer at the meeting where a multi-disciplinary team was discussing F75 reports—those which are written every three years to assess the progress of life sentence prisoners.

I chose to disagree, not because I thought the assessment was wrong, for Brian did not appear to exhibit remorse. I believed he had moved beyond that stage. How long can one expect people to go on showing remorse? When is it more than just a learned response, or appropriate response, to satisfy the needs of the report writer?

Brian had been in prison for a long time. He knew what to say, when to say it. We had spent many hours together and my initial revulsion of what this otherwise likeable man had done had long since passed. Or so I thought. Rereading his record, with its details of the offence, I was forced to question my own assessment. But I went with my heart.

How could I justify, or even explain my difference of understanding to my probation, and other colleagues? Brian was not particularly religious and only occasionally attended chapel, but what he was now manifesting in his life, was, I felt, repentance, not remorse. It is a distinction worth reflection. Is remorse any more than regret, or self-blame for an action? Something which can be acknowledged without having to think about giving up a previous way of life? Something which can easily lose its 'bite' with the passage of time and become merely an uncomfortable memory?

Repentance is something different. It is about 'metanoia', a reorientation of the personality, a renunciation of a particular way of life, or thinking. It may be the start of transformation, a radical change of perspective which does not require that the past be negated, or rejected, but which involves a new perception, a re-cognition of that past. And it is, I feel, more acceptable in the prison context than conversion, which too often can mean such a 'swing in the pendulum' that there is a chasm, a rupture, between past and present, with a refusal to accept the reality of that past.

Others were not convinced. Christian language and understanding is sometimes counter-cultural, and not understood, or accepted. Particularly amongst those who seek only to satisfy the desire for retribution. Six years later, Brian faces yet another review.

———————

> Rend your hearts and not your clothing.
> Return to the Lord, your God,
>   for he is gracious and merciful,
> slow to anger, and abounding
> in steadfast love,
>   and relents from punishing.
>
> (Joel 2: 13)

God may perhaps grant that they will repent and come to know the truth.   (2 Timothy 2: 25)

Do you not realize that God's kindness is meant to lead you to repentance?   (Romans 2: 4b)

———————

**God of mercy
our words express
our beliefs about you,
our understanding of
your grace and love
in the lives of all your people.**

**In our care for others
help us to be careful
in our use of language,
that we may show forth
your kindness, and through it,
lead people to repentance.**

RACE MATTERS ▥

J OHNSTON was in the Health Centre Treatment Room. His skin, scalded by boiling water mixed with sugar, hung from one side of his face, neck, and shoulder. His blackness, only skin deep; his burns and pain exposed and raw.

Later, in the quiet of the chapel, he spoke of what could only be described as a racist attack by another prisoner. 'Everyday of my life I been subject to abuse from white people. I've never set foot outside my front door one day without racist remarks.' But he steadfastly refused to make a complaint; 'It ain't worth it—I'd get worse than this probably.'

Johnston is an Afro-Caribbean prisoner, one of about 12 per cent who go to make up the prison population. Eighteen per cent of all prisoners, 18 per cent male and 25 per cent female, are from ethnic minority groups, representing a disproportionate number, given that 6 per cent of the wider community are from such minorities. Whilst one of the reasons for the high number of black female prisoners reflects involvement in the importation of drugs, and even when foreign nationals are excluded, the number of black people in prison still remains disproportionate. At the time of writing figures show that 9 per cent of British national male prisoners, and 12 per cent of British national female prisoners were black, compared with 1 per cent of British nationals aged 15–64 in the general population. Race matters.

Johnston, at 23 years of age, had been in trouble with the law for the first time. But he was no more likely to have committed an offence than a young white adult. Unlike his white counterparts, he was less likely to have been involved in the use of illegal drugs. But he was more likely to go to prison for his offence than a white person. Prison population statistics indicate that black people who commit offences are more likely to end up in prison than comparable white offenders. Yet black people coming into prison have fewer convictions than white prisoners.

No social inquiry report was prepared on Johnston. Of black and Asian defendants 37 per cent had no such report prepared, compared with 22 per cent of white defendants. Race matters.

Johnston told me of the many times he had been stopped and searched by the police in his late teenage years and until his imprisonment. Living within the Metropolitan Police area of London, where during 1994–5 302,691 people were stopped and searched, he was one of the 37 per cent from ethnic minority groups, one of 112,763. With his application for bail too, he had failed, and statistics show significant differences between white and black/Asian people granted this facility. Race matters.

Johnston's scars are deeper than the wounds I saw exposed. He feels he comes from a community which is disadvantaged, and which suffers disproportionately from poverty, poor housing, unemployment, and other forms of social deprivation. Race matters.

Whilst members of minority ethnic groups are over-represented amongst those dealt with by the criminal justice system, they are under-represented amongst the staff of most criminal justice agencies. In 1995:

- there were no High Court Judges from ethnic minority groups. Five of the 514 Circuit Judges, two of the 339 District Judges, 13 of the 897 Recorders, and nine of the 341 Assistant Recorders came from ethnic minority groups.
- there were no black Justice's Clerks. Seventeen of the 370 Deputy Clerk's, and 21 of the 1,470 Court Ushers were from ethnic minority groups.
- in 1995, four of the 248 Crown Prosecution Service staff in grades 1 to 6 (1.6 per cent), 90 of the Service's legal assistants (7.1 per cent), 77 of the 1327 executive officers (5.8 per cent), and 205 of the 2,384 administrative officers (8.6 per cent) were from ethnic minority groups.
- in September 1995, 2,223 (1.75 per cent) of the 127,222 police officers were from minority ethnic groups. Thirty-six Inspectors, eight Chief

Inspectors and one Superintendent were members of ethnic minority groups.

- in 1995, five members of the Prison Service's 1,020 Governor grades (0.49 per cent), 354 out of 19,325 prison officers (2.4 per cent) were from ethnic minority groups.
- in March 1995, 585 of the 7,905 Probation Officers (7.6 per cent) were from minority ethnic groups. The number of Senior Probation Officers had risen from three to 42, or from 0.26 per cent to 3.4 per cent. Eight members of ethnic minority groups were in management positions in the Probation Service, none of whom were Chief Probation Officers.
- in June 1995, 4 per cent of solicitors, and 6 per cent of barristers were from ethnic minority groups.

In some instances the figures have improved in recent years. None the less, race continues to matter.

Then Peter began to speak to them: 'I truly understand that God shows no partiality . . .'   (Acts 10: 34)

Those who say, 'I love God', and hate their brothers or sisters, are liars . . .'   (1 John 4: 20)

Lord, forgive us for the silence that
condones injustice
withholds forgiveness
disguises anger
prolongs quarrels
breeds misunderstandings
shows contempt
permits ignorance
kills love
expresses indifference
increases fear
makes barriers.

We pray for the gift of love
that we may trust and care for one another.

We pray for the gift of courage
that we may be bold in our work and witness.

We pray for the gifts of grace
that we may rejoice in our shared humanity.

We pray for the gift of faith
that we might believe we will be one.

We pray that you will hold us in your care
and make us wholly yours.

I saw Johnston a few weeks later, just before his transfer to another prison. He told me the scars were healing and his skin would eventually regain its natural colour. 'I don't want to be half black and half white, just to be me.' For him, as for most of us, race matters.

NOTE

I am grateful to the Penal Affairs Consortium for permission to use statistics from their paper *Race and Criminal Justice*, and to the Council of Churches for Britain and Ireland for the use of the above prayer. It originally appeared as part of the material for use in the Week of Prayer for Christian Unity, 1990.

CONFIDENTIALITY ▨

*B*ILL SALMON, *the Anglican Chaplain at Blundeston Prison, writes in this piece, and reflects in his prayer, on the issue of confidentiality. The seal of the confessional must always remain so, but there are many other areas relating to this matter which arise on an almost daily basis. It is rarely an area of conflict for chaplains, but the potential for it to be so remains. Blundeston contains long-term prisoners.*

As the Chaplain, I am leading a regular discussion group, where men are encouraged to 'be themselves', and to take 'time out' of the normal prison environment. Over the weeks I notice that one man regularly manipulates the group, despite efforts to prevent him doing so. We often find ourselves listening to his inappropriate jokes about women.

Later, I find myself having to write a report about this man. Reports are written when a prisoner is coming up for consideration for parole, or, every three years for a 'lifer'. His crime was of violence against a woman, but his reports indicate he has progressed well and causes no trouble in prison. The decision I have to make relates to the area of confidentiality. Do I reveal what I have experienced in the group, or do I allow it to pass without comment, in which case he may progress without further question towards release. Even if he agrees to disclosure, it changes the nature of the group. And prisoners need somewhere they can be relaxed and not feel 'watched' and tested.

Issues of confidentiality arise every day. Rarely major, sometimes trivial, they raise questions of how far chaplains are only the receivers of information, and not the sharers. Should a comment made in an unguarded moment, in a 'safe' environment, be passed to staff? Most often the answer will be 'no'. It's a risk, but as Jesus gave men and women dignity in his dealings with them, so in following Him we must hold carefully what men and women tell us as precious, and a gift between friends, not a commodity to be traded in the market-place.

> Lord, set a guard on our tongues.
> Help us to know when to speak
> and when to keep silence.
> In such a risky business when we make mistakes
> and should have spoken,
> by your love protect those involved.
> Be with all who write reports
> and in other ways handle
> intimate knowledge of others' lives.
> Make us ever careful
> with the precious gifts we hold.

ON DYING ▓

I N the hospice in adjacent rooms, Daffodil and Bluebell, lay the two men. John was a prisoner, handcuffed by one arm to his bed with a chain, discreetly covered with a rug by one of the two sensitive officers. In civilian clothes now, these two officers had been in uniform for some days attracting much attention and causing some anxiety for other friends and relatives, simply because of the implication of their presence. Prison regulations had demanded the wearing of uniform until relaxation could be sought on compassionate grounds.

The other man was a colleague, a member of the Christian Ministry Team, a Quaker who had been a dentist, then a Roman Catholic Deacon who had read Theology at Cambridge. A man of integrity and with a depth of compassion which meant he never failed 'to find something of God' in all whom he met. A man who loved and was loved, who had given of himself within and without the prison. The contrast was pronounced, despite their both being imprisoned by unconsciousness. John, chained to his bed, only to be 'released' with death; without family and with only one friend, himself a prisoner in another gaol. Dying alone, but ironically, in the presence of two unknown officers. Michael, surrounded by the love and gratitude of supportive family and friends, present with him over many months and through every stage of his illness. If he bore anything alone, it was because of choice. John had none.

The two officers asked if I would like to be alone with John. I sat beside his bed, his handcuffed hand in mine. I talked to him, but no reply came. I prayed the Lord's Prayer, slowly, deliberately, finding myself pausing as I said 'Forgive us our trespasses'—mine, and his. As I concluded, he clearly said 'Amen'.

To my words and prayers Michael made no audible response.

I was not to see either of them again.

Lord, Now lettest thou thy servant depart in
peace, according to thy word.   (Luke 2: 29—BCP Nunc Dimittis)

————————

**Lord, imprisoned by our fears,
by our limitations, by our humanity,
we seek you in all people
and in all places.
Be present with those who are dying,
alone, or surrounded by love.
Be present in the skills of those
who care for the dying;
in the care of all
who work in our hospices.
Be present in the hands of
those who share love.
Be present in those who
minister there in your name,
in word or deed,
in silent presence.**

Since writing this piece, a similar case, of a dying prisoner being
shackled to a bed, was widely reported in the media. Following an
apology from the Director General of the Prison Service, revised
guidelines were issued to staff involved in such sensitive situations.

DEATH ▨

J UST before eight o'clock in the morning as I handed in my 'tally' in return for a set of keys, the Senior Officer in the gate-house, said, 'Can you contact comms, Chaplain?' 'Comms' is the communications room, the hub of the information network within the prison, laden with sophisticated machinery and banks of monitors showing pictures of all areas of the prison, coming from innumerable cameras. The place also, where 'bad news' is received during the night.

In the room, accessible only after checks on my identity, I was handed the expected piece of paper, a Death of a Relative notification, with the first section carefully completed, the verification of details made through the hospital or local police, as necessary. Without such checks I could not inform a prisoner, given the number of 'hoax' calls which are received in the hope of distressing a prisoner, or getting a 'compassionate' visit, or even temporary release.

On this occasion I was satisfied and went to the wing where the prisoner was located and spoke with the officer on duty, seeking his insight into the likely reaction by the man, who was unknown to me. Simon was in a single cell, and with the agreement of the officer I decided to tell him in 'his own space'. The advice of uniformed staff is always crucial in such a decision, given the unpredictability and instability of some prisoners. There are times when it is necessary to give such bad news with the presence of an officer, and on neutral ground.

Knocking on the cell door and inserting my key at the same time, I was aware of the anxiety which always accompanies me at these times, no matter how often I have undertaken the task, one which everyone is very willing to pass to the chaplain! As I opened the door, and asked if I could come in, Simon's face registered 'the chaplain', early morning, and 'bad news', in an instant. I slipped the bolt, to prevent myself being locked in and sat on the one chair in the cell, as Simon sat on the bed. I tried, with sensitivity, clarity, and brevity to give Simon the news of the death of his grandmother. He allowed the tears to flow, unashamedly and unusually in this place where so many want to portray a hard-man image. We sat, the silence broken only by his tears and infrequent words. Sitting in openness, doing nothing but being present, is not easy. Sometimes it's possible here, sometimes it's not.

As time passed and the wing came to life outside the cell, Simon asked if he could attend the funeral, whenever it might be. In turn, I asked if she had ever acted *in loco parentis*? No, she had not. And so I explained that he must make application to the governor, but permission to attend a funeral is usually only given for a 'close' relative, for example, mother, father, sister, brother, wife, son, daughter, or a grandparent who had acted *in loco parentis*. Simon's disappointment was plain. I offered him the opportunity to come to the chapel at the time of the funeral, and for us to have some prayers together. Despite representations by the chaplaincy to Prison Service Headquarters to have grandparents included as 'close family', even when they have not acted *in loco parentis*, the situation remains unchanged.

As expected, his application had been refused and we sat, side by side, with God, in front of a lighted candle in the chapel, otherwise alone, just a few days later. Using some of the same prayers that were being used in the crematorium at about the same moment was helpful to him in his grief.

As we talked afterwards, he said he was glad he had not gone to the funeral, though he wanted to be there. The prospect of being handcuffed to two prison officers in front of his family and friends was not appealing. That afternoon, he had a visit from his parents.

If there is no resurrection of the dead, then Christ has not been raised; and if Christ has not been raised, then our proclamation has been in vain and your faith has been in vain.   (1 Corinthians 15: 13–14)

God of all consolation,
grant to those who grieve
the spirit of faith and courage,
that they may have the strength to meet the days to come
with steadfastness and patience,
not grieving without hope,
but trusting in your goodness;
through him who is the resurrection and the life,
Jesus Christ our Saviour.

(*A New Zealand Prayer Book*, adapted and to be found in *Human Rites*, compiled by Hannah Ward and Jennifer Wild, Mowbray, 1995)

A few days later, I saw Jim, a 'lifer' who had just exercised one of the few controls which he had left over his own life, and had taken it. His broken body lay before me. All our efforts to trace a relative or friend were to no avail.

In the cemetery, the undertaker's assistants lowered the coffin into the ground and withdrew to their car. I was left alone to say the funeral service, wanting to do so with dignity, for Jim's sake, yet uncertain as to why I should worry, and guilty because such a thought should go through my mind.

I knew that my role was representative, of the Church of which I was a member, of the Prison Service, of Jim's few friends in prison, of a community repulsed by his offences and who would not want reminding of his life. Yet I was deeply disappointed by my apparent lack of faith in the words of hope and resurrection, by my sense of isolation at a grave where even the undertakers men seemed symbolically to reject Jim's corpse. Even in death there was no escape from the stigma of being 'a prisoner'.

I don't know who it was, but someone once said, 'To work in a prison you need an infinite capacity for disappointment.'

But this I call to mind,
    and therefore I have hope:
The steadfast love of the Lord never ceases,
    his mercies never come to an end.

                    (Lamentations 3: 21, 22)

Lord, in disappointment
you give us hope,
in hope, love,
in love, your presence.
Enable us in honesty
to express our fear and anxiety,
our need to be restless
until we rest in you.
In your goodness
grant us wisdom and grace.

VICTIMS ▨

I RECEIVED the invitation unexpectedly, and initially I thought it had come to me by mistake. Would I attend the launch of SAMM in East Anglia? SAMM, Support After Murder and Manslaughter, a national organization dedicated to supporting and helping the families and friends of murder and manslaughter victims, were holding this very public launch in County Hall, also home to the Norfolk Constabulary HQ.

It was the first time I had been invited to any victim support group, and I wondered why. After all, I was one of those charged with caring for the offender, not the victim. When I met John Davis, one of the people behind the launch, he spoke of some offenders as victims too. His realism, and pain, were evident. He, and his wife Bernie had experienced the killing of their son, Jason, in January 1995 in Worcester. A young woman, also in the house at the time, had been seriously sexually abused.

After nine years of 'compartmentalizing' my ministry in prison, I now came face to face with some of those who were at the receiving end of the deeds of some of those I cared for.

John and Bernie's eloquence and commitment to SAMM could not hide the depth of their grief, the continuing pain and anguish a part of their physical presence. Bernie spoke of the choice which 'evil and wicked people have, but for the families of victims, there is no choice'.

Behind her, on a display board were photographs of some of the people killed by murder or manslaughter in East Anglia in recent years. As she spoke I realized I knew more than one of the men responsible. The colour photograph of two beautiful children, and their mother caused me particular emotion. I was regularly seeing the man who had killed them.

Never before had I faced victims, or their families, in this way.

Touched, deeply moved, and uncertain how to handle the feelings deep within me, I left, humbled. I could not help feel that somehow I was 'guilty by association'.

There are many groups committed to helping prisoners, ex-prisoners, and their families. Few exist to support victims, or their families. One speaker spoke of 'those who belong to this exclusive club, that no one wants to join'.

SAMM aims to:

- offer understanding and support to families and friends, who have been bereaved as a result of murder and manslaughter, through the mutual support of others who have experienced a similar tragedy
- raise public awareness about the effects of murder and manslaughter on families and friends.
- take up issues of concern arising out of the effects of murder and manslaughter.
- promote and support research into the effects of murder and manslaughter on society.

SAMM has over 900 members who have been bereaved through murder and manslaughter and between March 1995 and April 1996, some 290 new members joined the group for support, or to help others. Organizations such as SAMM and Victim Support provide enormous practical and emotional support for many distressed people.

Meanwhile, standing near the cross of Jesus were his mother, and his mother's sister, Mary, the wife of Clopas, and Mary Magdalene. (John 19: 25)

**Christ the victim
in your crucifixion
the innocent suffered.**

Christ the victim
in your pain
is our pain.

Christ the victim
in your despair
is our despair.

Christ the victim
in your confusion
is our confusion.

Christ the victim
in your isolation
you felt forsaken
by the Father.

In our isolation
help us to
share such feelings.
In sharing, to be supported.
In being supported,
to be restored.

Jason's killer received a life sentence, and is imprisoned. So too, Jason's family.

QUESTIONS ARISE 🔀

D AYS after the launch of the Support after Murder and Manslaughter Group, I sat in chapel trying to say morning prayer.

The endless round of activity within the prison, the demands, the uncertainty, the frustrations, the effort of listening, the expectation of speaking, were tiring and mentally draining. The man convicted of the manslaughter of his wife and the murder of their two children and whose photographs I had seen at the SAMM launch was in need of time and care, as were others.

As I sat trying to focus my thoughts on prayer, recurring questions ran through my mind: what am I doing in prison? What is the nature of ministry to the person who has committed such crimes? Why am I visiting this person? What can I do anyway? What do I have to say? Of what use can I be? How can I cope with what I hear? What is it that keeps me in this place?

Because it is here that I need God most. Here, that I recognize and acknowledge that need in a way that I have not done in my ministry outside. Here, where I have daily to seek Him, and sometimes, to find Him.

Alone in the chapel, with the hustle and bustle of 'A' Wing just metres away, with the noise of voices and the clanging of metal, I sit and try, once again, to pray. I fail to do so but I acknowledge my need, and ignore the written word before me.

As I sit the words of a hymn came to my mind, words from 'I the Lord of sea and sky'. I read them and pray them, especially holding onto 'I will hold your people in my heart'.

Acutely aware of the need for renewal of strength, vision, and calling, I am further helped by the words 'let the light of your love always shine in our hearts'.

God's love, not mine. I read the passage on which the hymn is based and left the chapel to see new arrivals, receptions.

———

Then I heard the voice of the Lord saying, 'Whom shall I send, and who will go for us?' And I said, 'Here am I; send me!'   (Isaiah 6: 8)

———

> **Lord, in the depths**
> **you are there.**
> **In the questions**
> **you are present.**
> **In the uncertainty**
> **you are certain.**
> **In our weakness**
> **you are strength.**
> **In our inadequacy**
> **you are love.**
> **In our failing**
> **you are vision.**
> **Lord, let the**
> **light of your love**
> **be present with us,**
> **let your voice**
> **call us once again.**

The prayer of another chaplain, in a gaol which makes mine look like a holiday camp, also reflected my mood. Pierre Raphael, then one of the chaplains in Rikers Island, a New York gaol which at that time held 13,500 prisoners, and in 1996, just over 20,000, wrote 'The Chaplain's Prayer for Breath':

Lord, in the prison I will not survive nor will I progress unless my eyes find you and rest on you.

Of course, I have the help of some of my friends, my sisters and brothers. We share a great deal, and not only our scars, our risks and our visions. All that is a very practical gift, not only useful but

indispensable. It would be very naive to come here without friendships, complementary, unproblematic relationships that are simply normal. Lonesome cowboys belong on the prairie, not in the prison.

But, Lord, I need the certainty of your presence when I pace the corridors, enter the cells and receive, day after day, like a blow on the head, the evidence of evil and of a world in fragments.

I need to believe in you through all that is life in me, so as not to know the defeat of your absence, for everything here, all the blows, cries and tears, seem to scream of it. I need your presence minute by minute. I have tried so many times to tell my imprisoned friends that freedom, which is such a huge, corrosive dream when it batters itself against the shadows, can revive the dead, even here, when we choose once and for all to depend on you; when we decide quietly, practically, correctly, daily, to be familiar with your words, with your life; when we choose the means to seek you, to accept our waiting, without brutalizing anything of the precious gift, the nourishment that is offered to us.

Finally, when you are Master, Shepherd, Friend in our lives, one stage is finished. Another opens to us, like a new universe.

Every day, before going in, before passing through the bars, remind me to take the time necessary to mobilize joy.

NOTE

'The Chaplain's Prayer for Breath', Pierre Raphael, *Inside Rikers Island* (Orbis Books, Maryknoll, New York, 1990), 28.

WHOLENESS AND THE
THERAPEUTIC COMMUNITY ▓

G RENDON PRISON is the only designated therapeutic prison in the
country. It is a Category B Training Prison which has 200
prisoners, of whom sixty are serving life sentences. Those not
serving life have an average sentence of seven years. It is a place where it is
expected people will develop their potential, and where they will change. A
critical part of the commitment of individuals to the therapeutic programme is
motivation, and the acceptance by each person of himself, and the need to care
for himself. This involves a quest for the truth about the self.

For those who have undergone therapy there has been a significant
reduction in reoffending rates and these have been lower than in those who
have not undergone therapy. Not all succeed, however, and a percentage of
men return to 'normal' prisons without having completed the therapeutic
process. No similar facility exists for women prisoners. Canon Keith Pound,
recently retired Anglican chaplain reflects on what it means to be a Christian
chaplain in this therapeutic community and on the need to seek wholeness.

Not many days go by without my having to think and pray about what
it means to be a chaplain in a therapeutic community, or, because little
or nothing is done without other Christian people in this place, what it
means corporately to be the Christian presence in such a place. Many
insights go into the quality of life we share together, and to which
many professional disciplines contribute.

The Christian contribution is not particularly valued for itself. Many
people think it to be irrelevant, outmoded, distracting, or positively
harmful. For a therapeutic community is little different from any other
community outside in the range of belief systems which are
represented in it by both staff and residents. Those who do seek to
exercise their discipleship in such a place have to face many
accusations, that they are using their faith as an escape from reality,

that they are refusing to face up to their actions, that they are falsely relying on supposed other-worldly resources instead of seeking to order their own lives, that they substitute some idea of quick-fix forgiveness for a realistic exploration of their own responsibility for what they have done to others. We pay the price daily for the distortions and misunderstandings which abound about the kind of new life Christians enjoy as members of the Church of Jesus of Nazareth.

Retreat into the 'spiritual' will not do. That simply reinforces the idea that many non-believers have, that we are laying claim to be working in some special sphere which is quite different from the ordinary concerns of psychotherapy and which is certainly not subject to any of the tests of efficacy used by those with secular presuppositions.

What we have to do is to recognize areas which we have in common and stand firm on the differences.

All of us in a therapeutic community are looking for the truth about people, however painful it may be. We need to see ourselves as we are and not as we have taught ourselves to appear. There is no shortage of stories in the New Testament about those who are challenged to drop the masks and let their true selves be seen. The woman at the well, not surprisingly evasive about her marital history, and also indulging in theological games, is also a searcher for the truth and brings others to the source of that truth. The thief on the Cross had a moment of disclosure which shows his real self, not just simply as a hopeless recidivist, but as one who is promised eternal life. Life in a therapeutic community involves a search for the real person and not just the one whose persona has been overlaid by years of rejection and who as a result has learned to be someone different from themselves.

We are all interested in change. Some Christians might want to use the word conversion, but it would not help. What is the motivation which brings about real change in people? Can disgust at one's past life, a growing awareness of what one has done to victims and loved ones, a sense that one has being playing a part, a comparison of experience with others who have faced similar problems, some increase in self-esteem, an enhanced capacity to communicate—can these processes bring about change? Yes, thank God, for many they do. But for others that will not be enough. They will want to examine, to revisit some nagging question about life's purpose; they will sense that human solutions are not all; that they have always had as a part of them a feeling for the God dimension, or they will find for the first time that they cannot make sense of themselves without it.

We are all interested in wholeness, although I find this word little used. Jesus' healing ministry illustrates again and again the interconnection between the different aspects of ourselves. Our guilt feeds our worries; our worries can make us ill; our illnesses feed our anxieties; our anxieties make us demanding and impossible in our relationships; the breakdown in our relationships make us more anxious; our anxiety can breed unreasonable and offending behaviour which feeds our guilt, and so, all too often, the whole dreary business goes on in a descending spiral of frustration which is all too familiar to anyone who works with those who have fallen foul of the law.

A healing ministry cuts through this vicious circle and introduces the possibility of newness and wholeness. 'Take up your bed and walk.' There is no need any longer to be dependent on the crutches and supports which have held back the disabled person from the right kind of independence and from being able to order his or her own life as a mature and responsible human being. Many interventions which can reverse the downward descent will come from the insights and processes of secular therapy, but finally for Christians wholeness comes only from the rediscovery of the image of God in that particular person through the work of the Lord.

But so that you may know that the Son of Man has authority on earth to forgive sins—he then said to the paralytic—'Stand up, take your bed and go to your home.'   (Matthew 9: 6)

Lord God, thank you that you mediate healing to men and women in many ways and through many professional disciplines. Thank you for the search for the truth, the understanding of ourselves, the awareness of what we have done to others and the possibilities of living differently which can be learned in a therapeutic community. Help us with humility and integrity to live out that wholeness of life which alone comes from the healing touch of Christ and in the power and inspiration of His Spirit.

ABSENCE ▓

ICK was not an attender at chapel, or any chaplaincy activity, but we met frequently. Our first contact arose as a result of his being referred to me by a psychologist, a colleague within the prison. She was concerned about the enormous guilt carried by this young man. He had been in prison for a couple of years, serving 'life' for the murder of a young child. Sigmund Freud said that people who feel guilt torment themselves for their bad behaviour without needing external judgement. Of the many people I have met in prison over eleven years, this was particularly true in Nick's case. Torment described his daily life. It was not physical, for he had been accepted by other prisoners. The anguish which he experienced was mental and spiritual. His torment was evident in his daily life, acknowledging as he did the horror of his offence. It was hideous. He never sought to provide excuse, to plead any sort of mitigating circumstance, but constantly wrestled with what it meant for him to be alive, and his victim dead.

Nick believed in God and over three years I tried to link his story with the greater story of God's pain. I could not.

Nick's belief in God was expressed through his sense of the absence of God in his life. Absence and presence are two aspects of the divine experience for many of us. Another prisoner, who was executed for his beliefs in the Second World War, was Dietrich Bonhoeffer. Whilst imprisoned he wrote: 'The God who is with us is the God who forsakes us (Mark 15: 34) . . . Before God and with God we live without God'.*

Nick was tormented by his guilt and by his feeling of God's absence, despite his belief. We tried to explore what it meant to experience the absence of that God.

R. S. Thomas, retired priest and poet, writes passionately of the silence of God, of his absence.

In the poem 'The Absence,' he writes:

It is this great absence
that is like a presence, that compels
me to address it without hope
of a reply. It is a room I enter
from which someone has just
gone, the vestibule for the arrival of one who has not yet come.

('The Absence', in *Frequencies*, Macmillan, 1978, 48)

For Nick, the resonance was acute.

> **God of presence**
> **help us to understand**
> **your absence.**
> **Help us to understand**
> **that in the absence**
> **you call us**
> **to know you.**
> **We hold before you**
> **our sense of being forsaken,**
> **that through it we may acknowledge**
> **that without you, we are without hope.**

NOTE
*Dietrich Bonhoeffer, *Letters and Papers from Prison*, ed. Eberhard Bethge (SCM Press, 1971) 360.

THE MINISTRY OF
RECONCILIATION ▨

W E sat side by side in the small chapel in the Prison Health
Centre. Robed to symbolize my representative priestly
role, or to hide my humanity, vulnerability, and confusion
over what I was doing?

A lighted candle on the altar, representing the light of Christ in dark
and broken lives.

Tom's life was badly broken, as were the lives of those who were his
victims. The woman he loved, and the child they created and for
whom, he said, there was no time for confession. Now, he wanted to
take upon himself their sin, as well as to express his own.

I hear many 'confessions', but few in the formal setting usually
associated with that word. Even in prison. Perhaps, especially in
prison.

Falteringly, I began with some words from 1 John 1: 8–9, associating
myself with Tom: 'If we say that we have no sin, we deceive ourselves,
and the truth is not in us. If we confess our sins, he who is faithful and
just will forgive our sins and cleanse us from all unrighteousness.'

Tom had prepared himself well for this moment, when he would, in
God's presence, make a humble confession of his sins. Hard as it was,
he had taken care to think about the way he wanted to express his
repentance. As I sat and listened, aware of our common humanity, I
thought of the great cost involved in forgiveness—for the person
confessing, God, and those called to embody it.

None the less, and despite all I have heard and read of people's
offences, I was ill-prepared for this catalogue of acts which seemed to
distort what it means to be human. But Tom, I felt, was not simply
seeking absolution for his sin. It was deeper and more significant than
that, and later, in my reading, I began to understand what it was. An
American Methodist, and theologian, L. Gregory Jones, in his book,

Embodying Forgiveness (Wm. B. Eerdmans Publishing Co., Mich., 1995, p. xii), writes, 'As such, a Christian account of forgiveness ought not simply or even primarily be focused on the absolution of guilt; rather, it ought to be focused on the reconciliation of brokenness, the restoration of communion—with God, with one another, and with the whole Creation.' He tells us that forgiveness is a 'craft', which Christians need to learn to embody. A 'craft' rooted in a Trinitarian understanding of God.

Tom's confession was, for me, another stage in that continuous learning and understanding of God's love, and of trying to gain skill in the 'craft'. For Tom, perhaps, it was the beginning of reconciliation.

> Then I acknowledged my sin to you,
>   and I did not hide my iniquity;
> I said, 'I will confess my transgressions to the Lord',
>   and you forgave the guilt of my sin.
>
> (Psalm 32: 5)

Almighty and everlasting God,
you hate nothing that you have made
and forgive the sins of all those who are penitent.
Create and make in us new and contrite hearts,
that, lamenting our sins
**   and acknowledging our wretchedness,**
we may receive from you, the God of all mercy,
perfect forgiveness and peace;
through Jesus Christ our Lord.

(*The Alternative Service Book, 1990,* Collect for Ash Wednesday)

PRISONERS' WEEK ▦

P RISONERS' WEEK was started in England in 1975, and Prisoners'
Sunday is the third Sunday in November, with the week
observed until the following Saturday.

It is an ecumenical observance and many churches throughout
England, Wales, and Scotland use the material produced each year. In
1996, for example, the theme was 'Dignity and Healing for All'. Based
on the concept of Restorative Justice the material was produced by the
Canadian Prison Chaplaincy Service, and added an international
dimension to the week.

The Prisoners' Week Committee is made up of prison chaplains and
other Christians working with prisoners and their families. The aim of
the week is to encourage all Christians to focus their thoughts and
prayers on prisoners, prisoners' families, victims of crime, prison staff,
and all working in related areas.

> **Lord, you offer freedom to all people.**
> **We pray for all those who are in prison.**
> **Break the bonds of fear and isolation that exist.**
> **Support with your love: prisoners, their families**
> **and friends, prison staff and all who care.**
> **Heal those who have been wounded by the activities**
> **of others, especially the victims of crime.**
> **Help us to forgive one another, to act justly,**
> **love mercy and walk humbly together with**
> **Christ in His strength and in His Spirit,**
> **now and every day.**
>
> (Prayer reproduced by kind permission of the Prisoners'
> Week Committee)

It is a week when many prisoners feel they are able to get involved in some of the events which take place. Ted is one such prisoner, and he wrote the following prayer for use during the week:

Heavenly Father, you see us for what we are:
men who are searching, and those who have found:
those driven by fear and those comforted by faith;
souls burdened by guilt and grief,
or lifted by love and companionship.

You know where we have come from:
cherished by a loving family and respected by our peers,
or from the fringes of society, unvalued and alone;
from lives of security and comfort, or from want and distress.

We have come before you in all our differences,
but united in our common desire to serve you in our daily lives.
Lord, captivate our souls and free us from sin;
surround us with your love and release us from loneliness.

We thank you for the prayers
and deliberations of Prisoners' Week:

Take me prisoner, Lord
And truly set me free;
Help me lay down my sword,
Then victorious shall I be.

TAKING LEAVE ▦

A NUMBER of times I have been surprised by prisoners saying to me 'After you left my cell', or, 'When you left the wing, there was a different feeling for a time, a sense of peace'.

We need to listen to this sort of comment, not because it makes us feel good as ministers, but because it contains a deep theological truth. It is right that our leaving is as good as our coming. For the way in which we leave can create a space for the work of the spirit of God; for God to be present in some new way. It is right there should be a difference when we have left. And that difference should encourage an intimacy with God, through his spirit.

Some chaplains will always offer a prayer before leaving a cell and through such prayer and presence the living God may be encountered.

Nevertheless, I tell you the truth: it is to your advantage that I go away, for if I do not go away the Advocate will not come to you . . . (John 16: 7)

God our Father
as your son prepared
to take leave of his disciples
 he promised the presence
of your spirit, the Advocate.
May we encounter your
spirit of love
and through it, your peace.

THE WORD ACROSS THE PRISON WORLD ▒

MOST prisons in England and Wales are fortunate in having a good relationship with the local branch of the Gideons. Operating internationally, this group, dedicated to spreading the word of God in the Bible, distributes millions of Bibles and New Testaments worldwide. Each year in the United Kingdom they are responsible for ensuring delivery to schools, hospitals, hotels, etc. One little-known aspect of their work is in prison, where they supply thousands of New Testament and Psalms each year.

Stories abound about the value of the Gideon Bibles and New Testaments. I want to include two stories, linked together in a common thread, but separated by thousands of kilometres. The first is written by the Revd Dr 'Mack' McFerran, an Interfaith Chaplain in Vancouver, Canada. Mack has ministered in fifty prisons in Canada, New Zealand, and the United States of America, during fifty years, and has regularly produced prayer material for those in prison. He has done so from a variety of faith perspectives. He writes:

Ben and I sat together on the side of his bed, in his cell. We had eaten supper together and now there was a time for fellowship. I sat fingering a leather-bound Bible, every book in it marked by a tab, page after page of verses underlined and with notes. Ben's Bible told the story of a man who had found God and in the process had found life.

Ben was doing two years, on the advice of a legal aid lawyer, for a crime he had not done. When he unexpectedly was sent to gaol the consequences were catastrophic. He lost his job and his family, and he felt there was no future, no hope, no justice.

He was reluctantly persuaded to attend chapel on his first Saturday in prison. Oblivious to the whole service, at its conclusion the chaplain handed him a New Testament. On the return to his cell he threw it at the toilet. When nature next called he picked it up and read a verse of comfort on its foreleaf—'I have set before you life and death, blessings and curses. Choose life.' In the moment it took to read that verse the hurting, the hate, the hopelessness fell away and Ben felt the Presence of God—a God of love who cares.

Ben read that New Testament from cover to cover, never finding those life-changing words from Deuteronomy 30: 19. Months later he was put on the garbage detail. He wondered about being a Christian, but continued faithful. One day while emptying the garbage a coverless book fell onto the ground. When Ben picked it up he found that it was a complete copy of the Bible. He hurriedly thumbed through it, finding that verse of salvation—'I have set before you life and death, blessings and curses. Choose life . . .'

The Bible I held in my hand was that precious book. He had bound it in brown leather and marked it prayerfully. He and I, with that miraculous book in my hand, started giving thanks to our Father of blessing, and prayed:

Heavenly Father, you have set before us choices in life.
Thank you for giving us eyes to see, ears to hear and
hearts to respond to those choices. Help us to remain
faithful to your Presence and to accept in joy your promises.
Through Jesus Christ our Lord.

John Hargreaves, formerly an Assistant Chaplain General in the English and Welsh Prison Service, recounts an occasion when he was making an annual visit to the Chaplaincy at Hull:

'You're the Vicar from Stafford aren't you?' The voice boomed across the landing bridge from what appeared like an overgrown bramble-bush on the top of a man some six foot four inches tall. I had just stepped out of the chaplain's office at Hull to go to the chapel.

'Well, I was about six years ago,' I replied.

The prisoner reminded me that we had met in the Segregation Unit while he was confined there for police investigations.

'I used to listen for your footsteps every day,' he went on. He then dashed into his cell and emerged clutching a rather battered, but clearly much read, Gideon Testament.

'You gave me this. Your visits and this book were my lifeline then, and I still read it every day.' For a second I felt proud, and then very humble as I remembered how often I would have been glad to give that visit a miss.'

So shall my word be that goes out from my mouth;
    it shall not return to me empty,
but it shall accomplish that which I purpose,
    and succeed in the thing for which I sent it.

(Isaiah 55: 11)

Lord, thy word abideth,
And our footsteps guideth:
Who its truth believeth
Light and joy receiveth.

O that we, discerning
Its most holy learning
Lord, may love and fear thee,
Evermore be near thee.

(Henry William Baker, 1821–77)

THE MENTALLY DISTURBED ▩

An inward, and involuntary groan was my reaction to seeing Peter again. It was only a matter of weeks since he had been discharged, and now he had returned. Diagnosed as having a personality disorder, and with a dependancy on alcohol, he is one of a significant number of people who constantly come and go from prison. So many seem to be caught in a seemingly, unending cycle of offending, arrest, and trial, followed by institutional detention or care—a process sometimes referred to as the 'revolving door' syndrome.

Peter, at least, has a home, unlike an estimated 15,000 in prison who claim NFA—'no fixed abode'.

In 1975, the Butler Report on mentally abnormal offenders acknowledged a significant number of people who were homeless, without roots, and often unable to live in the community without practical support and help. Butler wrote, 'Among this group are to be found individuals suffering from distinct psychiatric disorders, often personality disorder, chronic schizophrenia or organic psychosis, a number who are subnormal and many others on the borderline of mental disorder or dependant on drugs or alcohol.'

A 1991 study, 'Mentally Disordered Prisoners', led by Professor Brian Gunn, indicated that of those prisoners serving six months or more, 37 per cent of the male, and 56 per cent of the female sample had some form of mental disorder. Whilst acknowledging that there has been some criticism of Professor Gunn's methodology, the figures remain worryingly high. In a subsequent study he has shown that mental disorder is even more common amongst remand prisoners, with psychosis being diagnosed in almost six per cent of the sample, schizophrenia, psychotic, and delusional disorder in over five per cent, neurotic disorder in 19 per cent, and neurosis in 28 per cent. Neurosis and neurotic disorders were higher again amongst women prisoners at 43 per cent and 27 per cent respectively, whilst those with a psychiatric disorder and schizophrenia was lower than that found in the male sample.

In 1996, 746 prisoners were transferred to psychiatric hospitals under Sections 47 and 48 of the Mental Health Act 1983, a threefold increase since 1989. The figures fail to reflect that there are many others who are waiting to be transferred when places become available. The constraints operating within the National Health Service can mean that no bed-spaces exist at the time they are needed. In turn, this may lead to a breach of the time limit set for the transfer from prison to hospital.

The Chief Inspector of Prisons, Sir David Ramsbotham, writing in his first Annual Report (1966), said, 'There is particularly urgent need for increased provision for the care of those with mental health problems, who make up a larger proportion of the prison population than they would of any other group in the community. What is more, unless proper care is provided, prison can exacerbate mental health problems, which has a long term impact on the individual concerned and the community into which he or she may be released.' It might be appropriate to ask whether 'community care' will be adequate to deal with some of those released.

As the number of people in prison increases dramatically, so does the likelihood of prisoners being dispersed around the country, far from their families and support systems. This may adversely affect those who are mentally disturbed in particular. It would seem that Lord Woolf's 1991 recommendation for community prisons, whereby prisoners could be held in prisons near to their home, and which might have helped tackle some of these problems, seems unlikely to come about.

Many staff in prison feel ill-equipped to provide the sort of care which people such as Peter, and so many like him, are entitled to receive. As a consequence, staff anxiety may be heightened because of an awareness of the increased vulnerability of such people, producing a sense of helplessness mixed with hopelessness.

Then Jesus asked him, 'What is your name?' He replied, 'My name is Legion; for we are many.'   (Mark 5: 9)

Moved with pity, Jesus stretched out his hand and touched him . . .   (Mark 1: 41)

> God of wholeness
> your son encountered
> the disturbed in mind
> and body; in acceptance
> he showed your love
> and compassion.
> In your love be
> present in the lives
> of those who suffer
> anguish of mind,
> and in those who
> offer them care.
> Be present in their skills,
> that they might foster
> wholeness.

NOTE
I am grateful to the National Association for the Care and Resettlement of Offenders (NACRO) for permission to use information contained within their report *Mentally Disturbed Offenders*.

THE GAOL 'LOTTERY' ▦

T HE traditional image of justice is the statue on the Old Bailey, blindfolded, with the scales of justice in one hand and a sword in the other. Symbolizing impartiality, thoroughness, and the prospect of a fair trial, it is an enduring representation which captures much, but also misses much.

In 1986 I started to take a small part in the ministry of the chaplaincy team at Durham gaol, attending once a week. Nothing had prepared me for the huge number of people arriving in such a busy 'local' prison. But the abiding memory which I have of a gaol which served courts in many different areas of the north-east, is of the apparent inconsistency in sentencing, for what appeared to me to be very similar offences. It seemed 'pure chance', even a 'lottery'.

Ten years later, it seems that this geographical lottery continues. An analysis of cases in 1996 shows that people are seven times more likely to be gaoled in some parts of the country than in others. A person convicted of assault, burglary or theft is more likely to be gaoled in Chesterfield, Derbyshire, where 16.5 per cent were sent to prison, than in Wakefield, West Yorkshire, where the figure was 2.4 per cent.

The experience I had in the north-east of England suggested variations within the same area and the report shows this to be the case. Sunderland magistrates gaoled 15.3 per cent of convicted people, whilst in nearby Newcastle upon Tyne, the figure was only 5.7 per cent.

In some areas, such as Maidstone and Folkestone, Kent, a convicted person is more likely to receive a community penalty than in Blackburn. Yet, a person convicted of theft is three times more likely to be gaoled in Folkestone than in Blackburn.

Whilst magistrates will say that a wide range of factors must be taken into account in deciding on a sentence, there does appear to be widespread inconsistency in sentencing, with considerable effect on those convicted, their families, and their future in the community. For some people it can mean a minor inconvenience, a fine, a public reprimand which goes largely without notice. For others it can mean utter devastation, the loss of a job, an income, family and friends, and the pain and humiliation of imprisonment.

> **God of justice and integrity,**
> **we hold before you**
> **those entrusted with**
> **the responsibility of sentencing**
> **the convicted.**
> **Enrich them with**
> **a spirit of discernment**
> **that they may administer**
> **'the scales of justice'**
> **with mercy and impartiality.**

LIGHT BEHIND BARS ▨

I FIRST encountered the Prison Phoenix Trust when I was Anglican Chaplain of Wakefield Prison. At the time, the largest maximum security gaol in Europe, it held 700 men, over half serving 'life', the other half in excess of four years.

A number of prisoners had read, and been influenced by the book We're all doing Time, by Bo Lozoff (Human Kindness Foundation, 1985). Providing practical help and advice about meditation techniques, but not located in any particular 'religious' tradition, it was in steady demand. An invitation to the Director of the Phoenix Trust, who distribute the book, led to a record attendance of long-term prisoners attending a discussion group on its work and on meditation techniques.

Sr. Elaine MacInnes is the current Director of the Trust, a sister of Our Lady's Missionaries, and the first Roman Catholic religious to become a Zen master. For a time she taught meditation to dissidents in prison in the Philippines under the Marcos regime. Whilst there she saw the potential for prisoners to benefit from their experience of imprisonment.

In this piece she writes about one of the 1,650 prisoners with whom the Trust corresponds.

In some prisons, fear is almost palpable. The result is physical tension, both for inmates and prison officers. The Prison Phoenix Trust teaches some of the stretching exercises of yoga, another spiritual discipline, to help free the body from this bond, and to precede the actual meditation. We travel around the country giving workshops to staff and prisoners alike, and then prepare teachers to carry on the work. At the moment we support these teachers in more than seventy prisons. When I came to the trust four years ago, the first letter I opened was from an inmate called Paul in Norwich Prison. He had just seen our newsletter, and submitted a poem called 'The Strip Cell' for us to print:

In the strip I sat
Humiliated, dejected, depressed.
It seems that no one cares. Do they?
Well, it seems not. Am I forgotten?
I hear a jangle of keys
I bang, I shout, I swear,
It seems as there's no one there. Is there?
At last someone comes; my saviour from this
hell—or not.
What do I want?
The screw shouts at me
'Just a chat, Guv' I say meekly
'Not a chance lad' he grunts
Is this real or an illusion
Who knows or cares?

Over the past four years, I have come to know Paul rather well. He was born in Glasgow. His mother committed suicide when he was two years old, and the neglect and abuse he suffered at the hands of his alcoholic father led to his living in care in a series of homes, which inevitably ended in failure. He lived on the streets and learned a life of crime. His automatic response to any threatening situation was violence, and since the age of 14 he has been convicted of eight felonies. His behaviour inside prison had been equally destructive. He even attacked the prison visitor and broke his jaw. There is hardly a protest possible that he has not employed in an effort to vent the inner damage and pain.

One could only wonder whether meditation was having an effect on this young man. Then on his twenty-fourth birthday two years ago, he wrote a different sort of letter, reflective about his violent past and present, and sad to think that that might be all the future held for him too. 'I wish I could get my head straight,' he wrote. I encouraged therapy as an adjunct to his meditation, and eventually he came to Grendon, the country's only therapeutic prison.

From the start, his letters were different. He was speaking of 'Malcolm' and 'James' and 'Tim', explaining to me in the visitors' room later that they were the prison officers and governor. I remarked that it was good to learn that prison officers had names! Paul responded with a smile: 'And they call me Paul, too!'

Part of his healing was dependent on a reconciliation with the prison visitor who had been his victim. By the time he came to Grendon, his jaw had healed, and so had much of Paul's anger. It was a time of forgiveness and understanding for both, an experience Paul will not easily forget.

He is now in his last month in gaol. He has had his first home leave of three days, visiting his girl-friend and setting up a room where he will live. He wants to work 'helping people'. He wrote that he reported back in prison 45 minutes ahead of time, and that the prison officers seemed very pleased with his progress. He ended his letter 'I'm very pleased with myself too.' He has been given two names of people to whom he can go when he becomes confused or angry. I feel Paul now has a chance.

————————

But I have calmed and quieted my soul,
   like a weaned child with its mother;
   my soul is like the weaned child that is with me.
O Israel, hope in the Lord
   from this time on and for ever more.

(Psalm 131: 2–3)

God, Father of us all,
you see the suffering of your children.
You see our loneliness, our sense of separation,
and our sometimes despair.
Help us to use these situations
to come to a realization
that we are never alone,
that you are closer to us
than we are to ourselves,
and that in some mysterious way
we don't have to be anyone else,
or anywhere else, to find
a deep meaning and the possibility
of change in our lives.
For all of this lies hidden in our 'now' moment,
because we are your children,
and you are a caring Father.

NOTE

The central part of Sr. Elaine's narrative first appeared as part of an article in *The Tablet*, in August 1996. She later wrote the prayer for inclusion here.

BAPTISM ▧

I HAVE rarely baptized a prisoner, not primarily for theological reasons, though I have always encouraged short-term prisoners to wait until they become part of a worshipping community outside the prison. But also, because there has been little demand! David Bosch in Transforming Mission, *reminds us that 'People are never isolated individuals. They are social beings, who can never be separated from the network of relationships in which they exist. And the individual's conversion touches all these relationships.' Baptism must always be contextual and about transformation, not just satisfying people's needs.*

In this piece, submitted by a colleague, and to which I have added a prayer of my own and one from the Franciscan Service Book, Celebrating Common Prayer, *the joy and sense of new life contained within the baptism service is in stark contrast to the situation awaiting the prisoner on release, highlighting the words of Bosch.*

Christopher was a tall sixteen year old, with a mop of uncombed hair. He was polite, agreeable and wrote impressive letters with perfect spelling. His father had left his mother when he was two years old. His step-father threw him downstairs and broke his arm before he was five years old. Christopher lived in twenty-six different children's homes before he was imprisoned. He settled into the young offender institution quickly and enjoyed coming to chapel because he felt loved, and the chaplaincy volunteers from outside churches took an interest in him.

Two years into his sentence he asked me if he could be baptized. I prepared him, and some weeks before the service he asked if I could find his mother, and invite her to the service. He had not heard from her for over three years. Through the network of volunteers she was found almost a hundred miles away, invited to the service and collected on the day.

It was a great occasion. Christians from around the country had answered my request in the prayer-letter for cards of greeting, and there were over eighty. The volunteers turned out in force, five clergy robed and took part, and many of his mates were present for a splendid service.

During the tea party that followed, Christopher's mother assured me that when he was discharged from prison just two days before Christmas, he would go and live with her It was the best baptism present she could give him.

Seven days before his discharge Christopher received a letter from his mother in which she told of a new relationship with a man in the north-east of the country, and there would be no place for him after all.

As many of you as were baptized into Christ have clothed yourself with Christ.   (Galatians 3: 27)

> God of transformation,
> in baptism you confer
> new life in Christ.
> Grant that all who are
> baptized into his name
> may be enabled to keep
> the covenant they have made,
> and boldly confess him as Lord
> of life; and respond to the
> prompting of your Spirit.

Almighty God,
in our baptism you have consecrated us
to be temples of your Holy Spirit:
may we, whom you have counted worthy,
nurture this gift of your indwelling Spirit
  with a lively faith,
and worship you with upright lives;
through Jesus Christ our Lord.

(*Celebrating Common Prayer*, Collect for
Epiphany 1)

HIGH-PROFILE CASES ⬚

F EW cases in English legal and penal history have evoked as much
public reaction as that of Myra Hindley, Ian Brady, and the infamous
Moors murders. In the piece which follows, Suzanne Moore, who
writes for the Independent newspaper, raises profound questions for those
concerned with such high-profile cases. She also refers to the killing of James
Bulger, a child who had not reached three years of age when he was murdered
by two 10-year-old boys in 1993.

Suzanne writes from a humanitarian, and not a religious-faith perspective,
but she has given me permission to add a prayer. The piece first appeared in
the Independent in February 1997, following the decision of then Home
Secretary, Michael Howard, that Myra Hindley should never be released. It is
thought there are about twenty people in British prisons who have been
similarly informed that they will never be released.

Myra Hindley will never be free. Michael Howard has told her this
officially. It will take a brave home secretary to release this woman and
we do not expect such bravery from Michael Howard. Why should
this woman be free when the parents of the children she helped
murder have had to live with a life sentence of grief? Why doesn't she
do the decent thing demanded in countless tabloid editorials and
commit suicide?

There is of course more than one way of taking a life and we have
taken Hindley's. The average life sentence is fourteen years: she has
been in prison more than three decades. No one seriously believes she
will be a danger to anyone if released. She is a 54 year old woman with
osteoporosis yet we refuse to see her this way. Instead she is forever a
peroxided evil tart who didn't have the grace to go mad as Brady did; a
woman who defied the basic instincts of her gender. It's possible
according to the certifiable Dr Raj Persaud, a consultant psychiatrist

employed by the *Daily Mail*, that upon release she could even meet another Brady. Once more she could become the accomplice of a man obsessed with Nazism and sadism. Once more she could . . .

So Hindley will die in jail and the anguished parents of her victims still raw with pain will declare this 'the best day of their lives'. The judge at her trial is reported as saying that he didn't believe she was beyond redemption but politicians, not the judiciary, have decided that she is.

Her supporters—including Lord (Loopy himself) Longford—appear to have done her more harm than good by their very unworldliness. How would you feel, the mob screams at this 91-year-old man, if it were your child? How would you feel? Wouldn't you want to kill them? Destroy their life as they have destroyed yours? That's what it is to be human and by implication the likes of Longford are as devoid of human response as Hindley herself.

Yet Longford, sustained by his Catholicism, is one of the few public figures who are not embarrassed to talk about forgiveness or at least its possibility. Forgiveness does not make for sexy headlines. No, all these years later we prefer headlines like 'Evil Myra's Lesbian Love Calls are Axed' or 'Brady: don't set Myra Free' or 'Rose West and Myra Hold Hands'. We prefer to leave Hindley in jail, locked forever in the terrible events of the mid-Sixties.

She struggles in her letters to explain herself but never shows enough remorse or understanding of what she has done. What would enough be? She is cold, manipulative, detached, analysing herself as if she were only ever an iconic media representation, never a woman of the flesh with blood on her hands. As time goes by she becomes increasingly articulate and we understand her less and less, condemn her more and more. In 1978 it was thought she should serve a shorter sentence than Brady. In 1990 the Home Secretary that she should serve a whole life sentence. Have the sentences been rejigged as her release date draws nearer or have we become less forgiving? How has this woman moved from being possibly redeemable to being utterly beyond redemption in the course of 30 years? If we do not begin to understand this then the lynch mob rules indeed.

During the trial of the boy murderers of James Bulger, young men gathered at the court. Blake Morrison in his book *As If* (Granta, 1997) describes them thus: 'The men . . . had come wanting to kill the kids who killed the kid, because there's nothing worse than killing a kid.' Morrison's troubled and troubling book attempts to understand what happened at that trial, how children were put on trial as if they were adults by adults who should have but didn't let themselves know better.

By the anniversary of James's death those sad, fat little 10 year olds had already joined the pantheon of 'Britain's most reviled killers'. The spectacle was raised that they may be freed in their twenties and already a campaign has been mounted to keep them in prison forever. Various Bulger relatives had vowed to kill the two upon release, just as the relatives of Hindley's victims promise to murder her.

Surely if we have any faith in rehabilitation which after all is still one of the professed aims of incarceration, then children have more chance of being rehabilitated than adults, yet if we continue to judge these boys as adult murderers then no forgiveness is possible.

It is difficult to talk about forgiveness from a secular view-point, we don't have enough markers. We are merely proclaiming our faith in an idea. We sound far too wishy-washy, far too liberal. Yet as Morrison writes, 'Only a culture without hope cannot forgive—a culture that doesn't believe in progress or redemption. Have we so little faith in ourselves we can't accept the possibility of maturation, change, cure?'

The answer is that we have little faith indeed. While the language of therapy crops up everywhere—the concepts of repression, denial and projection are commonplace—our belief in actual change is small. Tinkering with one's psyche may be positive but the chance of deep and meaningful change we feel remains remote. So we sit in judgement, closing down on people whose worlds closed down long ago.

I fear it is already too late for Hindley. Her case has already been taken out of the hands of the judiciary and become obscenely tied to political posturing that does nothing constructive for anyone, least of all the red-eyed parents of her victims who must relive their trauma time and again for the rest of us. Hindley is right to argue that she has now become a political prisoner. But it is not too late for Bulger's killers, and to bracket them alongside her and Brady is another kind of crime altogether. If our justice system is to be based on the feelings of the bereaved alone then we may as well hang every killer and be done with it.

It is unfashionable in these days of law and order to insist that prison must serve some purpose beyond that of simply punishment, but we must. Is to align oneself with loony peers, judges and other professionals who support Hindley's release to mean that one has been duped by a scheming middle-aged woman? Is it too much to ask for a penal system that is no longer fuelled by the lust for revenge alone?

We have a choice as to whether we are ruled by our baser instincts or whether we believe it is possible to rise above them. In our hearts we may never accept that those individuals who have taken the lives of children are ever able to do this. Collectively, however, we must have faith in that possibility, for without it all sentences become death sentences.

Forgiveness does not mean forgetting or excusing hideous crimes, it means only that we believe in the potential for change, that we choose life over death, that faced with horrific acts and evil monsters, we endeavour in whatever way we can to remain human. If this is asking so much then let each and every one of us stand in the enormous queue of those who are prepared to do to Hindley what she did to others, to join the lynch mob. Then we might know what she knows and we might know what it is to be no longer human.

It seems right to append a long section of Psalm 51, a Prayer for Cleansing:

Have mercy on me, O God,
　　according to your steadfast love;
according to your abundant mercy
　　blot out my transgressions.
Wash me thoroughly from my iniquity,
　　and cleanse me from my sin.
For I know my transgressions,
　　and my sin is ever before me.
Against you, you alone, have I sinned,
　　and done what is evil in your sight,
so that you are justified in your sentence
　　and blameless when you pass judgement.
Indeed, I was born guilty,
　　a sinner when my mother conceived me.
You desire truth in the inward being;
　　therefore teach me wisdom in my secret heart.
Purge me with hyssop, and I shall be clean;
　　wash me, and I shall be whiter than snow.
Let me hear joy and gladness;
　　let the bones that you have crushed rejoice.
Hide your face from my sins,
　　and blot out all my iniquities.
Create in me a clean heart, O God,
　　and put a new and right spirit within me.
Do not cast me away from your presence,
　　and do not take your holy spirit from me.
Restore to me the joy of your salvation,
　　and sustain within me a willing spirit.
Then I will teach transgressors your ways,
　　and sinners will return to you.

(Psalm 51: 1–13)

For if you forgive others their trespasses, your heavenly Father will
also forgive you; but if you do not forgive others, neither will your
Father forgive your trespasses.　(Matthew 6: 14–15)

God of humanity
in a world of violence
we acknowledge our capacity
to corrupt your image.
Foster the sorrow that heals, and
through your grace restore
your likeness within us.
By your holy spirit
may we know the joy and gladness
which praises,
that we may take our place
among your people,
forgiven and restored.

(Adapted from the prayer following
Psalm 51 in *Celebrating Common
Prayer*.)

Almighty and everlasting God,
you are always more ready to hear than we to pray
and to give more than either we desire or deserve.
Pour down upon us the abundance of your mercy,
forgiving us those things
    of which our conscience is afraid
and giving us those good things
    which we are not worthy to ask
save through the merits and mediation
of Jesus Christ your Son our Lord.

(*The Alternative Service Book 1980*, Collect for Easter 5)

RESTORATIVE JUSTICE ▓

ELSEWHERE *in this book (e.g. in Victimization), I have called on Christians concerned about the criminal justice system in general, and the prisons in particular, and their respective failures, to seek for alternative models. In this piece I want briefly to introduce the concept of Restorative Justice. I am grateful to the Religious Society of Friends (Quakers) for their permission freely to use material contained in their 1995 paper,* Repairing the Harm: Friends and Restorative Justice. *It is a concept which has potential application in many areas of life, including our personal relationships.*

The current system of criminal justice primarily sees the breaking of the law as an issue only between the offender and the state, ignoring the relationships involved in any offence—the victim, the victim's family, the offender's family, and the community. Restorative Justice asks us to do something to mend that which is broken, to heal the hurt, and to remove the causes of harm. It asks us to use healing as an alternative to retribution and punishment. I feel it is worth quoting one piece at length and I have added a prayer with which to conclude.

Retributive justice dictates revenge, not healing, and demands punitive sanctions instead of addressing the needs of the victim, the offender and the community. If the intended use of alternatives to prison is to restore justice and peace in the family, in the community and in societies throughout the world, careful consideration must be given to how these alternatives are used.

Seeking justice according to a restorative model leads to a new set of assumptions:
· offenders accept responsibility for their criminal behaviour.
· there is recognition of the harm done to the victim
· there is opportunity for reconciliation through direct interaction between victims and offenders.

- offenders are not punished, but supported to repair the harm done, and to seek help for their problems.

Research into the needs of victims indicated that most victims desire recognition of the harm done to them, restitution from the offender and a commitment that further crime will not be perpetrated by the offender. In restorative systems of justice, we move away from vengeance to address the well-being of victims.

Restorative Justice respects the basic human needs of the victim, the offender and the community. The administration of justice, according to the restorative model, includes the active participation of people directly involved and affected by the criminal activity. Settlements provide redress to the victim and make it possible for the offender to fulfil agreed obligations.

Restorative Justice provides one alternative model. To achieve it would require an enormous, radical, and fundamental shift. It reflects biblical justice, and is worth consideration.

And what does the Lord require of you
but to do justice, and to love kindness,
and to walk humbly with your God.

(Micah 6: 8)

Restore us, O God;
let your face shine, that we may be saved.

(Psalm 80: 3)

God of healing
you have called us to
'do justice and love mercy';
to heal the hurt,
to mend the broken
relationships of our lives.
Fill us with the hope
which reflects your
grace and love;
which seeks to repair the harm
we have caused,
and to restore us
in your peace and salvation.

IV
PRISON STAFF

THE CHAPLAIN GENERAL ▨

T HE *Chaplain General to Her Majesty's Prisons is a priest in the Church of England, and usually an Archdeacon. He is licensed by the Archbishop of Canterbury to be the 'shepherd' to Anglican prison chaplains in England and Wales. He is responsible for the selection and deployment of 123 full-time and many part-time Anglican chaplains. The Chaplain General operates from Prison Service Headquarters in London, and has a ministry to staff at that level as well as to chaplains. He spends a great deal of time visiting prisons and overseeing the ministry of chaplains within prisons.*

The Chaplain General, at the time of writing, is the Venerable David Fleming, a former part-time chaplain to a Borstal, now redesignated as a Young Offender Institution. In the following two narratives he draws on his diverse experiences at Headquarters, to place God at the very heart of daily life.

Part of the ministry of all chaplains is to pray regularly for those connected with prisons, and many chaplaincy teams have a monthly prayer-letter which is widely distributed to prayer-partners. Prisoners, staff, Prisons Board members, Ministers of State, need prayer. We do it, and we do it gladly. Usually it passes apparently unnoticed but recently I had two examples of the fact that the ministry is appreciated.

A Christmas card from a member of the Prisons Board with a hand-written message '(David) thank you for your prayers in '96, please continue for '97'. And then, a chance meeting in the street with a retired Director of the Prison Service, who said, 'I still talk about you and the Chaplaincy Headquarters Team beginning your day by praying for us as we went about our work—how much I valued that'.

In St Paul's letter to the young Christian, Timothy, he writes, 'First of all I urge that petitions, prayers, requests and thanksgivings be offered to God for all people.' How great a ministry that is and how easy it is for all, old, young, prisoner or free, to be involved. Remember how Terry Waite, from the depth of his captivity felt the prayers of the faithful to be a light in his darkness.

Heavenly Father who through thy Son Jesus Christ hast taught us, saying, Ask and it shall be given you, seek and you shall find, knock and it shall be opened to you: Give us grace now to ask in faith, according to thy Word, to seek only what is agreeable to thy holy will and to knock with patience at the door of thy mercy until our petition is granted and prayer is turned to praise for the glory of thy holy name.

(Frank Colquhon)

CALLED TO SERVE

The selection of Anglican chaplains for full-time prison chaplaincy takes place through an assessment centre. This is a series of exercises designed to give the assessors an opportunity to see potential chaplains from many angles. The exercises involve preaching a short sermon, writing a pastoral letter, chairing and taking part in a committee exercise, an interview in a role play, and facing the questions of the assessors.

All are revealing, but none more so than the role play. Recently the theme was 'Breaking bad news'. The potential chaplain was asked to break the news of the death of a near and beloved relative of a prisoner. It seemed he might have an opportunity to give comfort and hope when the prisoner asked, 'Do you believe in God?', but the candidate pushed him away by saying, 'Yes I do but I don't want to talk about that now.'

Whatever else they do chaplains must never forget they are Ambassadors of God. Using every opportunity to proclaim the Good News of Jesus Christ. Always by 'being' but quite often by 'doing' and 'saying'. We thank God for these opportunities and for his all embracing presence and love.

Christ be with me, Christ within me
Christ behind me, Christ before me
Christ beside me, Christ to win me
Christ to comfort and restore me
Christ beneath me, Christ above me
Christ in quiet, Christ in danger
Christ in hearts of all that love me
Christ in mouth of friend and stranger.

CALLED TOGETHER ▦

THE historical fact which has led to the Church of England chaplain being appointed as 'the Chaplain' to a prison establishment is an anachronism, and seen by some as an affront to ecumenical understanding, and inter-faith co-operation. Fraught with potential difficulties it has, all too often, led to ministry being seen as the responsibility of one person. Every prison has a Roman Catholic and a Methodist chaplain, though strictly within the understanding of the Prison Act 1952, they should be referred to as 'prison ministers', along with representatives of other Christian, and living-faith traditions. Such an expression, however, simply devalues the contribution of ministers of all faith-traditions, and of the concept and understanding of ministry as a whole.

Henri Nouwen, in his book, *In the Name of Jesus* (Darton, Longman & Todd, 1989), explores the future of Christian leadership. He uses the analogy of ministers as failed tight-rope walkers who have discovered that they do not have the power to draw thousands of people; that they do not make many conversions; that they do not have the talent to create beautiful liturgies; that they are not as popular with the youth, the young adults, or the elderly as they had hoped, and that they are not able to respond to the needs of their people as expected. Despite this, many in ministry feel they should be able to do it all and to do it successfully. The rampant individualism which is so much a part of our competitive society is not alien to the Church, or the chaplaincy.

Shortly before he died, Henri Nouwen wrote, 'We have been called to be fruitful—not successful, not productive, not accomplished. Success comes from strength, stress, and human effort. Fruitfulness comes from vulnerability and the admission of our own weakness.'

Such an understanding has had a profound influence on the way in which I have sought to exercise my ministry in prison and I have been privileged to share that ministry with others who think in a similar way. It seems from the Gospels, that Jesus saw ministry as more than individualism. In Mark 6: 7, where he sends the twelve out in pairs there may be the grounds for a collaborative approach to ministry, with the implication that we cannot bring the 'good news' on our own. Throughout the years I have been part of three chaplaincy teams, I have seen the radical difference which ministry as part of a team can make. We recognize that it is better for us, and at times easier, to pray together, rather than separately; that it is easier to share the spiritual task; that it helps to share the pain as well as the joy, and that it produces a challenge. Through ministry together, it is easier for others to recognize and accept that we do not come in our own name, but in the name of the Lord who calls us.

In the words of Mother Julian of Norwich, 'If I look at myself, I am nothing. But if I look at us all I am hopeful; for I see the unity of love among all my fellow Christians. In this unity lies our salvation.'

I ask not only on behalf of these, but also on behalf of those who will believe in me through their word, that they may all be one. As you, Father, are in me and I am in you, may they also be in us . . .   (John 17: 20–21)

> God our Father
> you have called us to be your pilgrim people.
> Through the work of your Holy Spirit
> draw us ever closer to you and to one another.
> Together may we pray and worship,
> together may we work and rest,
> together share our sorrows and our joys.
> As we travel onwards
> towards the unity for which Christ prayed,
> show us the way
> and give us the grace and the courage to follow it.

NOTE

The prayer is adapted from one used in the 1992 Week of Prayer for Christian Unity material, and published with the permission of the Council of Churches for Britain and Ireland, then the British Council of Churches.

LIVING-FAITH TRADITIONS ▨

I T was Ramadan, the month during which Muslims fast from sunrise to sunset. During that time I was frequently in the prison at sunset, and the Imam invited me to 'break-fast' with him. Together, we shared, in the presence of God, sometimes in silence, sometimes in dialogue, always with respect for each other's faith tradition. Shortly before I left that prison he invited me to his home for a meal. I was the first non-Muslim person to enter his home and to eat with him during his adult life.

The Sikh Visiting Minister regularly made me welcome at the *langar* (which literally means, the common kitchen), to share in the food served after worship in the gurdwara (temple). The gurdwara in the prison was a designated multi-faith room.

The Rabbi was always keen to discuss common issues relating to theology. The Buddhist Visiting Minister taught meditation techniques to some long-term prisoners, and his personal 'sense of peace' was palpable, and appreciated by all he met.

So many different people of living-faith traditions are represented, and contribute to the life of so many prisoners and staff; to our understanding of God, and the richness of cultural and religious diversity in the spiritual aridness of the penal system.

It has been a privilege to encounter such people, to stand with them, to learn from them, and to reflect on what it means to be a Christian in dialogue with those whose faith is also 'living', and whose call to ministry brings them into prison.

My own understanding of faith and my relationship with God has benefited from being exposed to the faith and understanding of these people and their traditions. I have come to appreciate what David Bosch describes as the 'abiding paradox of asserting both ultimate commitment to one's own religion and genuine openness to another's'.

I am the God of your father, the God of Abraham, the God of Isaac,
and the God of Jacob.   (Exodus 3: 6)

God of Abraham, Isaac and Jacob,
we give you thanks
for the richness and
diversity of faith.
With all your people
we open ourselves
to your living Spirit.
Enrich us with the ability
to encounter and to share;
that we may deepen
our understanding of your
presence, your love
and your grace,
in those made
in your image.

BUSYNESS ▨

PRISONS are incredibly busy places and local prisons, where
people are received from the courts (magistrates, county and
high), receive thousands of receptions and discharges every
day. Throughout the prisons in England and Wales there is constant
movement of prisoners. All day people are moving from one place to
another, to workshops, to court, to education, to groups, to be
interviewed, to see a solicitor, to see a visitor. Meetings of one sort or
another are taking place, prisoners are being reviewed, suicide
prevention strategy is being planned, budget cuts and their implications are being faced. Prisoners are seeking attention, from main grade
officers, governors, teachers, probation officers, chaplains.

There is constant noise, and my office, adjacent to some telephones
and to the reception area, is often filled with the sound of abusive
language, as suggestions are flung at relatives or friend, the police, or
Group 4 staff bringing men to, or taking them from the prison. Some
of the suggestions hurled are physically impossible, but the noise is
penetrative.

In the midst of this at times frantic environment, those who
minister in prison may be easily tempted into 'justification by
busyness'. The immediacy of ministry in prison makes demands which
create an illusion for our busyness, our usefulness, our indispensability.
Within the safe walls, the security of our busyness, the demands of our
role, the self is often denied, and God too.

We need to be confident enough to step out of the security and
safety of our role as chaplains, with our prescribed ways of thinking,
subtly influenced by prisoners, staff, government policy, the Church.
Only then can we be truly creative, prophetic, concerned with
wholeness. But the demands are huge; time for prisoners, staff,
meetings, administration, the wider Church. In the midst of this

busyness we need space to acknowledge our basic lack of fulfilment, when we allow the spirit to engage and challenge us.

'God is the still point at the centre,' wrote Mother Julian of Norwich. Privileged as I was last year to celebrate the Eucharist in her 'cell' in St Julian's Church in Norwich over many months, I became increasingly aware of the need to centre my life on God. Perhaps a start would be to look at the diary, to create time to be with God as readily as we create time for people or routine administration.

Be still, and know that I am God!

(Psalm 46: 10)

Almighty God,
you have made us for yourself,
and our hearts are restless
till they find their rest in you.
Teach us to offer ourselves to your service,
that here we may have your peace,
and in the world to come may see you face to face;
through Jesus Christ our Lord.

(*The Alternative Service Book 1980*, Collect for Pentecost 18)

PROBATION STAFF ▩

T HE Probation Service, which in 1996 had 596 officers seconded
to the Prison Service, is the only statutory agency that
consistently works with offenders before, during, and after
custody.

In recent years probation officers working in prisons have focused
on two distinct areas of work, first, reducing the risk of reoffending
and preparing prisoners for release and, secondly, giving practical
support to prisoners, their relatives, or dependants. The two fit well
with the second part of the Prison Service's statement of purpose: 'Our
duty is to look after them (prisoners) with humanity and to help them
lead law-abiding lives in custody and after release.' Probation staff have
the potential to play a significant role in helping the Prison Service to
achieve this aim. The two areas are part of the concept of 'throughcare', which is the basis of the partnership between the two services.

Probation staff bring a huge number of skills to their work in
prisons, acknowledged by John Hutchings, Her Majesty's Inspector of
Probation, in a report published in 1996. It is a list worth quoting in
full, for the benefit of those who are unaware of the work done by
such people in prisons throughout England and Wales:

- 'skills in the assessment of dangerousness and risk, coupled with an
  appreciation of the surveillance/support structures necessary to
  reduce crime and protect the public from sexual and other violent
  offenders.
- skills in the identification and assessment of offenders' behaviour,
  motivation and likely future behaviour, especially on return to the
  community.
- skills in working with offenders who display various types of
  abnormal behaviour, e.g. addictive, compulsive, aggressive and
  violent.

- experience and knowledge of the criminal justice system: roles of various agencies; powers of the courts; parole; experience gained through working relationships with judges, magistrates, police and the Crown Prosecution Service.
- knowledge of the family courts structure and system, especially care procedures, divorce, parental responsibility, residence and contact.
- knowledge of community resources and agency responsibilities, including specialist offender provision.
- experience of licence supervision and throughcare systems.
- skills in analysing behaviour pertinent to work with offenders in prison or the community, e.g. stigmatisation and discrimination, alienation, scapegoating and institutionalisation.
- skills in using and evaluating different methods of intervention, such as group work programmes and special projects.
- training in the use of social work methods: e.g. cognitive and social skills, individual and family counselling, therapeutic and problem-solving group work techniques, behaviour modification, conciliation and mediation.
- report writing, training, negotiation and inter-agency skills.'

Sir David Ramsbotham, Her Majesty's Chief Inspector of Prisons for England and Wales, writing in his first Annual Report in 1996, highlights the vulnerability of Probation Departments, '. . . 48% had cut back their probation officer complement. And this is only year one of a three year programme, during a population explosion that looks certain to exceed the availability of new places . . .'

The figure of 596 probation officers working in prison in 1996 reflects a reduction of 50 on the previous year, with further reductions identified for 1997, and subsequent years, in some places. Such reductions have led to considerable anxiety amongst probation staff and their managers about their ability to deliver a quality service to the benefit of prisoners, prisons, the courts, and the public.

If financial cut-backs mean the work cannot continue at its existing level, let alone develop further, it is likely to have a negative impact on the overall performance in prison establishments, and on the lives of prisoners. Should this happen, the behaviour of some prisoners may be affected and their preparation for successful release be diminished. Many prisoners, their families/dependants, and staff in prison, have benefited from these skills and any diminution of their availability will be to the detriment of society.

At present a review of the link between the Prison and Probation Services is taking place and this may lead to some form of integration in a Correctional Service. Such a service could help provide a 'seamless link' between sentencing and supervision, better preparing prisoners for a return to the community.

. . . and who is my neighbour?   (Luke 10: 29)

Lord, your Son
visited humanity
in all its suffering and need.
Inspire Probation Officers
with love and compassion;
encourage them amidst
anxiety and uncertainty.
Give them wisdom and patience
in their care for your people.
And as we give thanks
for their skills and dedication,
we acknowledge our call
to show your love in our lives,
and in our care for one another.

LIVING WITH RISK ◼

ALL *who work in prison are at risk, of physical, psychological, or emotional harm. Staff face daily encounters with difficult and unpredictable people. Constant vigilance is necessary, but risks have to be taken as part of each working day, every encounter. Julia tells her story, and concludes it with a prayer.*

When I was working as a probation officer I was responsible for seventy prisoners on one wing of the prison. Many were serving 'life', and all were serving over four years, and the offences they had committed were serious—murder, rape, armed burglaries, drug offences, and sexual assaults.

My task was varied and I never completed it. I had to prepare reports on each of those men for their Annual Review (called Sentence Planning). I had to address which of the Groupwork Programmes each should be doing to look at the causes of their offending. I had to plan and run some of the group-work. I had to liaise with other prison staff about problems. Sometimes I had to see families when they were visiting and I had to keep in touch with the home probation officers. In order to achieve this I was required to make early contact with each prisoner as he came on to the wing—from another prison or from another wing of our prison. In that way I tried to have personal knowledge of all those I was working with.

I was aware that there was a new prisoner on the wing who I had not seen and I was on the point of making an appointment to see him. Then, at a daily 'surgery' (when we saw prisoners to deal with any immediate needs) he came into my office—a converted cell—as if to ask me a question. I felt relieved that I had been saved a job. It did not turn out like that. Within seconds he had launched a violent attack on me and I was only saved when my screams were heard.

The turmoil that followed was made worse by excessive press interest because of my husband's job* and the identity of the prisoner. Hate mail followed, and it took me many weeks to recover. Indeed there are some parts of me that will never recover.

The Sunday after the attack I was in church, and we sang 'To God be the Glory'. I had to leave when we started to sing the line 'The vilest offender who truly believes, That moment from Jesus a pardon receives'. It challenged everything that had happened to me and I thought it made nonsense of most of my experience as a probation officer. WHY?

When some of the strongest feelings about the attack on me had lessened I wondered if I could face seeing my attacker to ask why he had done it. I could not stop being a probation officer and wanting to find out the causes of the crime and to try and do something about it so there would be less chance of it happening again. I didn't see him. One of the chaplains did, and said that there was no hope of any change, and the hurt would be mine.

So what about forgiveness? Have I forgiven him? Is he repentant? I do not know. That is for others to work for, on my behalf.

What I do know is that I was supported by so many colleagues and friends that I felt that God was there upholding me. Indeed, I have made new friends as a result. I have also learned how it feels to be a victim and know that it is an insight I can bring to my own work that was not possible before.

Some prisoners tell me that they will never reoffend. They may not have apologized, or in Christian terms, 'repented', but they want to lead a crime-free life. Does God forgive them? It is a very hard question to answer. Especially for me, because as a probation officer I have to make an assessment of the 'risk' each offender poses, and, believe me, sometimes it is a gloomy picture, far removed from the story I have heard from the offender!

I am still working as a probation officer, and still have hope that the message of forgiveness and repentance might, for some at least, be of real meaning in the way they conduct their life in the future.

We are afflicted in every way, but not crushed; perplexed, but not driven to despair; persecuted, but not forsaken; struck down, but not destroyed; always carrying in the body the death of Jesus, so that the life of Jesus may also be made visible in our bodies.   (2 Corinthians 4: 8–10)

————————

Give us true repentance;
forgive us our sins of negligence and ignorance,
and our deliberate sins;
and grant us the grace of your Holy Spirit
to amend our lives according to your holy word.

NOTES
*Then an Archdeacon, now a Bishop in the Church of England.

The man tried for this attack on Julia was found not guilty of attempted murder, but guilty of false imprisonment. Already serving four life sentences, he was given an eight-year sentence to run concurrently with his existing terms.

DISCIPLINE OFFICERS ▓

I T is not uncommon to hear people refer to prison 'warders'—
sometimes in a pejorative way. The term 'warder' was last used
officially in 1921.

The term used since that time is 'officer' and this is more usually
'main grade' or 'discipline' officer.

The use of the word 'discipline' is interesting, given its etymological
links. The root is the same as that used in the word 'disciple' and is
about learning. It has at its very heart a connection to hope, linking as
it does to the future, not to the past. In the current recruitment
brochure for prison staff, it states: 'Prison work is not for the faint-
hearted: it requires imagination, humanity, optimism and courage.'
Optimism, learning, and hope all link together in the daily life of those
who work in our prisons, in any capacity, but they are especially
needed by the men and women who 'walk the landings', engaging
with prisoners daily. Some 26,000 of the 40,000 staff employed in the
Prison Service are officers. All of them receive three months' training
which includes a nine-week residential course at the Prison Service
College.

To prepare for prison life they are exposed to a wide range of
subjects from racial awareness and interpersonal skills, to search
techniques. They need them all. As a recently appointed officer Viv
says, 'It can be unpredictable unlocking the cell of a man who has been
locked up for over twelve hours; stressful dealing with the demands of
some who are in prison for their inability to curb their demands; tiring
being constantly vigilant, being aware of what is happening, who is
speaking to whom, who is manipulating, bullying, dealing; conscious
of the physical threat which underlies so much of prison life.'

It is a hard place to be and the success of the Prison Service is that
discipline officers, and others, go on doing such a good job with

prisoners, but it is not easy. Viv recognizes this: 'I can't believe I can make much of a difference; so many prisoners are manipulative, dishonest, trying to use me, and yet they have potential to be something different, which needs developing. Many staff find it hard to leave the job at the gate when they go home, 'I find it hard to get things and people out of my head,' she says.

Frustration can also creep in, particularly in a local prison where prisoners constantly come and go, some staying for very short periods of time, others for many months. Viv acknowledges the difficulty of doing anything significant with people in so short a time, yet, as a Christian, she feels she can utilize even the briefest of opportunities to affirm and value many of those with whom she meets. 'Most of the time it's an interesting, but very different job. There are times when it's boring and threatening, but it can be rewarding, just occasionally. Before I started to work here I had a neutral attitude to prisons, now I have a passion for them and believe I'm doing something worthwhile. I just want people outside to know what's happening inside.'

> **Lord, it's a hard place to be,**
> **an uncomfortable place**
> **a frustrating place**
> **a stressful place.**
> **A place where encounters**
> **are unpredictable,**
> **not always what they seem**
> **and often surprising.**
> **We give you thanks**
> **for the dedication**
> **and care of staff**
> **as they serve our prisons.**
> **We ask for the gifts of**
> **optimism, patience, and hope**
> **that we may do**
> **something of your will.**

GOVERNORS ▒

U NDER the Prison Act of 1952, every prison must have a governor, a medical officer, and a chaplain—the 'Holy Trinity' of the Prison Service as they are sometimes called! In the harsh economic climate of the late 1990s, with increasing emphasis on applying business and organizational theory and concepts, there has been a sea-change in the way in which the role of the governor is perceived. The man, or woman, entrusted with responsibility for the everyday running of a prison, must now combine an array of abilities ranging from management expertise to entrepreneurial flair whilst managing substantial budgets in the face of 13.3 per cent cuts and an increasing number of people in prison. It calls for considerable skill and personal resource.

Increasing devolution and responsibility to governing governors, from a diminishing number of people at Headquarters, has led to greater autonomy and to some governors seeing themselves as 'managing directors' of companies. For even a medium-sized prison will have a budget of some 10 million pounds. Ironically, whilst devolution is present in many areas, the simple replacement of a member of staff, or a reallocation of finance, has to be referred 'up'.

Set against an uncertain political background, governors have to juggle the often conflicting demands of security; the increasing lack of accommodation for an increasing number of people; reduced resources—financial and in personnel terms; raised expectations from prisoners in areas such as work, time out of cell, visits; and the potential risk of disorder as an expression of dissatisfaction, whilst trying to provide solutions which are in keeping with concepts of justice and humanity.

Such demands may well point to the need for a debate about the purpose of imprisonment and about policies which should be in the best interests of victims, potential victims, offenders, and their families. It must be of concern to many people that the philosophical basis on which the prison system should be based needs revision.

Governors have to respond to myriad demands, and policies, many of which seem to ignore any concept of 'wholism'. Increasingly, the recommendations made by Lord Justice Woolf following the riot at Strangeways Gaol in 1990, are being ignored because the resources are not there to implement them, or have been diverted to pay for increased security measures. Home leave, now called resettlement leave, has become increasingly hard to get for some prisoners, making it more difficult for them to reintegrate into society. The concept of community prisons, in which prisoners should be held in prisons as near to their home as possible has been a non-starter. Every day, hundreds of prisoners are moved around the country in an effort to match available places with people. Little if any consideration can be given to their needs. Prisoners have had a succession of restrictions imposed on them, including the amount of property they may have in their possession, access to their private cash, more frequent searches, mandatory drug-testing and the earned privileges and incentives scheme, which has meant they have to earn some of what they had before as part of the regime. Even the rule entitling prisoners to at least one hour of exercise each day has been altered to half an hour. The fundamental concept of justice for prisoners, such an important part of the Woolf recommendations, seems to have become 'a nice idea, but . . .'

Governors have to 'prioritize' the relative merits of disparate needs and benefits, weighing, for example, education and probation provision against security improvements or treatment programmes. They are 'between a rock and a hard place', and many are paying a high personal price through stress-induced illness. In a *Sunday Times* report in September 1996, the morale of governors was said to be so low that of the 1,100 in post, about 25 per cent had applied for redundancy. As one said to me recently, 'We are weighed down by the immorality within the system, and the undermining of our personal beliefs.' As the Reverend Christopher Jones, Theological Adviser to the Prison Service Chaplaincy Advisory Group has written of the Prison Service, 'it is de-moralized, and de-moral-ized'.

A Service which proclaims people 'to be its most valuable asset', needs to be reminded of the value of each of those individuals. Staff find it extremely difficult to treat people with justice and humanity if they feel they are not themselves being similarly treated.

Lord,
we hold in your presence
all who are called to be
governors in the Prison Service.
We pray that they may
have the gifts which
are necessary to
encourage those
who live and work
in prisons to achieve their potential;
to manage conflicting demands,
and to put the needs
of individuals at the
heart of their work,
through justice and humanity.

In times of despair
give them hope;
in times of anxiety
give them strength;
in times of despondency
give them perseverance;
in all life, vision.

EDUCATION ▨

F OUR *interrelated short stories provide a glimpse into the world of prison education. Creatively crafted, they reflect the imagination and care of Ben Butler, the teacher who wrote them. Ben has an infinite capacity to care for the marginalized, to seek out their inherent potential and to stand alongside them through their experiences. Each story is based on someone he has known. A Christian, his faith is reflected in his ability to be creative in every context, even, as we hear, in the midst of cut-backs and a diminution of the important work done in this field. After the four stories, I have added a prayer.*

WAYNE

A hundred and fourteen admitted offences, fourth custodial sentence. Father and older brother convicted and currently serving sentences.

For everything created by God is good, and nothing is to be rejected.   (1 Timothy 4: 4)

We did numeracy today. That's sums, really, but if you're thick and don't think like me you don't do maths you do numeracy. The bloke teaching us was wearing the same shoes he had the last time I was in doing a two for commercials. Sad shoes, I'm telling you. Couldn't be bothered doing the work so I had a go at him. Told him I was thick and always had been—they told me so at school—and always would be. Thinking does my head in. He just smiled. Not laughing at me, like, just friendly. Told me I wasn't thick at all. Just lacked confidence, he said. Maybe I was scared of thinking, scared of thinking things through, he said. Told him straight, I did. Not lacking in confidence, was I, four floors up on the roof of the warehouse and coppers' dogs waiting for me down below. He nodded, saying that he wouldn't like to be in my shoes. So how much do you get for teaching us lot then, I asked. Enough, he said. Not enough for a decent pair of shoes, I laughed, pointing down at his manky Hush Puppies. Wouldn't like to be in your shoes. Everybody laughed at him. Told him I always wore best Italian leather on the out. I make a couple of hundred an hour doing over warehouses. He wasn't impressed. Said that wasn't much. Got angry at that—so I had a right go at him and we all gave him some stick but he just wrote it up. Wrote my three hundred quid with his coloured pen. Then he asked how much bird I got. Told him. He wrote up my time, then started to do this sum—nice and slow so I didn't feel stupid and could keep up. We worked out how many working days there were in my sentence. Then we divided the bung I made by the length of time I got. Came out at less than two quid a day. Got a hell of a shock, seeing it up there in blue and white. Two quid a lousy day. Scared me. Makes you think, though, dunnit?

Before that sudden journey none is wiser in thought than he needs to be, in considering, before his departure, what will be adjudged to his soul, of good or evil, after his death-day.   (Bede's DeathSong, 735 AD)

ROBERT

Homeless, single and inadequate—drifting into petty crime and heavy drinking.

Full of doubt I stand,
Whether I should repent me now of sin
By me done and occasioned, or rejoice
Much more that much good thereof shall spring,
To God more glory, more good-will to men
From God, and over wrath grace shall abound.

(John Milton, *Paradise Lost*, Bk. XII. 437–8)

Come on, come on. Get them open. I hate this bit, waiting for them to open the gates. Over a hundred years old, these gates. CCTV cameras are new. Just think, on the other side, when I get through, there'll be friends, familiar faces. I'll be sorted. Loads to do. Lots to catch up on. Who's doing what. All the gossip. All the news. I always get this buzz at the gate. Come on, come on. What's the hold up? Oh, it's the screws coming back from the Mess. Did a spell in the Mess on the friers. That little woman from education said I did her chips just the way she likes them. Always thanked me, proper like. Got me roped in on a Food Hygiene course. Did it. Got the certificate. Then she mugged me again, got me to do a Health and Safety course. Got that too. She didn't talk much, but really listened. That's how I ended up going to the AA group and started to be honest about my drinking. Kept on at me, though. So I started to go to evening classes. Didn't know I was good at art. And the history was interesting, too. She said I should go down to the college when I got out and carry on. Me? At college? I laughed. She just nodded and gave me the name and phone number of a teacher she knows there.

Come on, come on. Open these gates. I'm buzzing. Through those gates and I'll be back with people who care, people who take the time to get to know me. That little woman from education always called me by my first name. Six hundred of us coming and going and she always remembered my first name. All the teachers the same. Great, things are moving. Here we go. Open, sesame. They're closing the gates behind me. I'm back—back in a world where there's food, a welcome, and plenty to do, friends and people who know your name.

Can't wait to get through Reception, get my kit and onto the landings. Might even get the same old cell. I didn't make it down to the college—this time. But I'll apply to get onto classes. Finish that picture of the barn owl. Back inside. Just like coming home.

> With such certainty ascended He,
> The Son of Man who deigned Himself to be:
> That when we lifted out of sleep, there was
> Life with its dark—and love above the law.
>
> (Denis Devlin, *Ascension*)

JOHN

Risk-taking entrepreneur. Imports fine wines.
Sentenced for five specimen charges of VAT evasion.

Cast thy care upon the Lord,
And He shall nourish thee Himself.
When I cried to the Lord,
He heard my cry.

(Traditional verse, after à Kempis)

At public school they said—after this, one shall be equal to anything one might encounter in later life. They were not quite right. The bullyboys and the food in here would be no match for the miseries of the Lower Fifth. Still, stiff upper lip. That's my motto. The family motto is longer, and in Latin, but amounts to the same thing. Of course, I refused to have absolutely anything to do with my people when I came into prison. Right thing to do. Frightful shame and all that. Simply couldn't face the parents. No visits. No letters. Then that lady from education came along to see me—just like Matron used to see the young boarders in their first week away from home. Decent enough type, but I told her I spoke four languages and had enough of the classics to last me a lifetime. Had her down as a sort of WRVS wallah, meals-on-wheels for the mind. We talked, and she advised me to keep in touch with my family. Visits were important, she stressed. Keep in touch with the loved ones. No need on my part, I told her. For their sake, she replied. Thought about it. Dammit, she was right. Wrote to them that night.

Rather afraid I've been a bit of a fool all round. Had a chat with that education lady. She asked me how was my Italian. They asked me if I had any Albanian. Wonder what the old trout's up to. Asked her for a book on cheese. Said she'd oblige. Sure enough she came the next day. Exactly what I wanted, together with a guide to setting up in business. Bookkeeping and simple accountancy. Useful stuff. Signed up for a course they run for the self-employed. Pity they didn't teach me that years ago. I believe we will cover VAT too. Ironic, really. I can quote yards of Horace but go into a blue funk with figures and accounts. She said she'd introduce me to software packages for spreadsheets and stock control. Never had patience for all that nonsense before. Know better now. I'll be steering clear of fine wines next time round, though. Go for continental cheeses. Wonder if HM Customs whack excise on Emmental. I'll ask that lady from education. She's bound to know.

The parents are coming tomorrow. I'm so glad. I do hope the pater doesn't do his Sandhurst stunt and inspect the prison officers as he walks in.

As, O God, we believe and hope for the good things of eternity, grant that we may so use the transitory miseries of this life as to obtain the permanent felicity of the next.   (Thomas à Kempis)

THE TEACHER

'It's going to be tricky providing for that Albanian deportee. Still, we manage it with the Ethiopians, the Romanians, and those four Turkish inmates up on the 3's landing. I'll see the landing officer and ask for a cell change before bang up. Get him in with John. They both have a little Italian between them. Well, it's a start. Oh, and I mustn't forget that book on cheese. So glad he made it through the first week. Often his type stoically fall on their swords. He's off the at risk list, and has signed up for the business skills course. I believe he's expecting a visit soon. His mother took it all very badly, I gather.

Wayne is a bright young man. I wonder where he'd be now if he'd had John's chances. Too soon to suggest he does a numeracy exam, I think, but he should eventually. Next month, perhaps. For so many of them it's a fear of failure, but for Wayne it's fear of success. Proven, measured intelligence is an uncomfortable burden for those whose plea is always ignorance. Exposes them to a greater sense of responsibility. Pity so many have to do the painful parts of growing up inside prison.

Robert is back. Seemed almost relieved to be back here. Dreadful fact is that this is his home. His whole way of life built around the overestimated comforts of prison.

The wing is down after the suicide last week. I've proposed a strategy of seeing all prisoners for an informal briefing and settling-in session every morning. Screen out the disturbed and the vulnerable, but everything costs and the sniffer dogs and the CCTV eat into the budget. Cutting the pencils in half should stretch our capital a little further, but it won't bring back the two music teachers.

Last month's exam results were excellent—so rewarding and motivating for the men here. They have such low expectations, such low self-esteem. As much failed by early learning experiences as failing within them, I'm sure. We don't have the luxury of a hidden curriculum here, we just make sure we deliver the provision with extra support, care and love. Trouble is, the men initially find this more difficult to grasp than the percentages, gerunds, and trigonometry. Harder for them to learn that they merit and need such care.

> Domine non sum dignus.
> (Lord, I am not worthy)

Education in prisons contributes positively to the dynamic security, safety, and care of prisoners. It plays a key role in addressing their offending behaviour; challenging their low self-esteem; assessing their untapped potential and assisting them to prepare for the challenges and opportunities on their release. It is therefore both curious and dismaying to discover that most education departments in prisons have suffered financial cut-backs of up to 50 per cent in 1997—and in the larger establishments up to 80 per cent.

Note: concern about the cut-backs in the provision of education has been voiced by Sir David Ramsbotham, Chief Inspector of Prisons, and by his predecessor, His Honour, Sir Stephen Tumim. It is estimated that at least 56 per cent of prisons have made cut-backs in their education departments. As is clear from the above narratives, education staff can play a crucial, and enabling role in the life of some prisoners, helping to bring about change. Education provides an environment in which there can be a real sense of achievement, of progress, of moving forward, in a place where life, and time, seem to stand still for so many.

Now when Jesus had finished saying these things, the crowds were astounded at his teaching, for he taught them as one having authority, and not as their scribes.   (Matthew 7: 28–9)

Christ the Teacher,
in your presence the people were
'astounded' at your teaching.

We give you thanks
for those who are
called to be teachers,
to exercise the creativity
which opens minds and hearts
to other perspectives,
other ways.

Be present through
their skills of mind and imagination,
that they may inspire and encourage,
through vision and freshness of thought,
those with whom they sit.

Bless and nurture their contribution
to truth, love, and the development of potential,
and in so doing, may lives be transformed.

HEALTHCARE ▨

ON average, 10 per cent of the people in prison, currently about 6,500, request to see a doctor or nurse each day. Certainly higher than the consultation rqte in the wider community, a number of factors may apply. Thirty one per cent of the prison population have medication prescribed compared with 19 per cent of the general population. Prisoners cannot have access to 'over the counter' medication for minor ailments, as they would outside prison. Even getting something for a headache may require medical involvement. More people in prison are likely to smoke—81 per cent, compared with 38 per cent outside; or to report a long-term disability, particularly musculo-skeletal and respiratory systems—46 per cent, compared with 29 per cent.

As has been noted elsewhere in this book (The Mentally Disturbed), prisoners are more likely to be diagnosed with mental illness or disorder. These mental illnesses or disorders may be of major concern and could include psychoses such as schizophrenia, and psychosis brought about by other problems such as substance abuse, personality disorders, and neuroses, including depression and anxiety.

Robin is a Prison Service nurse, with a background in psychiatry, who works in a busy local prison where thousands of people are received and discharged each year. He writes about some of his daily life, as he seeks to interact with people who are prisoners, and patients.

Prison Service nurses are a relatively recent addition to the professions working in the Prison Service. Generally, Prison Service nurses work alongside and are interchangeable with prison officers, who have undertaken a nine-week course to equip them as health care officers. Together with doctors, the community psychiatric nurse, dentist, visiting psychiatrists and pyschologists, we are all part of the multi-disciplinary provision continually available to ensure the daily routine and effective management of the people for whom we are responsible.

Part of my role, and that of other healthcare staff, is to be able to work within a variety of locations within the prison, performing specifically identified tasks. An overriding obligation is that we should always be available to respond to any emergency situation, when the need arises.

One task is to provide a health screen assessment for all new prisoners entering the prison from the courts. I always attempt to receive every person before me in a non-judgemental manner. I try to acknowledge the human being, not a faceless criminal. Based upon the information that I am able to gather during the routine, comprehensive physical and mental assessment, I decide where the person should be located within the prison. Ordinarily, someone presenting no prominent health problems will be located on normal location. Alternatively, if a person is in obvious need of further observation, recovery, or treatment, immediate admission to the Health Centre will be arranged.

Always conscious of those who may present as being at risk of self-harm, or suicide, I carefully assess such people. If necessary I will initiate the opening of a Self-Harm registration document which will then accompany that person to each location, including any further appearance in court. Only when that person is no longer considered at risk will the document be closed.

Many of those coming into prison, especially for the first time, are deeply anxious about their situation and whenever possible I try to give them as much information about the routine as I can, often having to use simple and precise language. But it does help some people.

It is an environment which demands constant observation, vigilance, sensitivity, and a willingness to respond to the demands of some demanding people. It is physically and mentally demanding and there is a constant tension between the application of nursing skills and security and discipline procedures. Assessment and treatment has to be balanced with the locking and unlocking of prisoners, with the restrictions imposed by a prison environment, even within a Health Centre.

It has its rewards, however. Norman was known to be a hard man. Demanding and uncompromising, he frequently sought to intimidate prisoners and staff. When he arrived in the Health Centre this pattern of behaviour was obvious from the start. Over time, and with care and patience, I was able to explore with him some of his demanding traits. Eventually it became clear that his wife and newly born daughter might provide a way to get alongside this man, to provide motivation for potential, and positive, change. The birth of his daughter had provided the opportunity for him to express his own sense of a lack of love through most of his life. Her birth was such an overwhelming event for him that, as we unpeeled the layers of his pain, he wanted to share his exhilaration with other people. New life, in this case, gave new life.

Recently, I have become involved with a new, innovative unit within the prison, the Relapse Prevention Therapy Unit, or RPTU, providing a sixteen-week, comprehensive programme of multiple approaches to drug-taking. The course aims to help people to improve their self-awareness, self-esteem, and their understanding, in an effort to help prevent them relapsing into the world of drugs. All of the prisoners, and we can take nineteen at any one time, are volunteers, men who want to face up to their addiction and if possible, to put it behind them as they look for an alternative life-style. As a nurse, and a therapist, this is the sort of healthcare for which I trained. In a prison environment where so much seems so negative, this Unit is a ray of hope.

He looked around at them with anger; he was grieved at their hardness of heart and said to the man, 'Stretch out your hand.' He stretched it out, and his hand was restored.   (Mark 3: 5)

God of restoration and wholeness,
we give you thanks
for the men and women who
work with those in prison Health Centres.
In the midst of the demands,
the anger, and frustrations
of difficult people,
may they hold to their calling
of care and compassion.
In your mercy
grant them patience, understanding,
and the gift of healing and restoring
body, mind, and spirit.

Almighty and everliving God,
whose Son Jesus Christ healed the sick
and restored them to wholeness of life:
look with compassion on the anguish of the world,
and by your healing power
make whole both men and nations;
through our Lord and Saviour Jesus Christ,
who is alive and reigns with you and the Holy Spirit,
one God, now and for ever.

(*The Alternative Service Book 1990,* Collect for 8 before
Easter)

V
CONNECTED GROUPS

THE BOARD OF VISITORS ▨

A ROUTINE telephone call, regular, but not frequent. 'Could you see John Mills on "B" Wing? He doesn't know what to do about his child and he needs someone to talk to about the situation.' Pat is a member of the Board of Visitors, a group of about thirteen voluntary lay members, two of whom must be magistrates, and appointed to every prison, including those in the private sector, and all young offender institutions in the country.

Members are appointed by the Home Secretary and have an important role in monitoring the fair treatment of prisoners on his/her behalf, and as representatives of the wider public, in whose communities prisons are placed and in whose name prisons are run.

The principle of independent inspection of prisons in this country dates to Tudor times, and members of Boards of Visitors have a right of access to any part of a prison, at any time. The Board is expected to raise matters of concern with the prison governor, or the director/controller in a privately managed prison, or with the Prison Service Area Manager for that prison. If necessary, the matter may be taken to the Home Secretary.

Board members are expected to hear any complaint made by a prisoner, satisfy themselves as to the state of the prison premises, the running of the prison, and the treatment of prisoners. In addition, they must enquire into and report on any matter of concern which the Home Secretary asks them to investigate; bring to the attention of the governor any issue they consider important; inform the Home Secretary of any abuse which may come to their attention.

Whilst all of this might seem quite far removed from the everyday concerns of prisoners, Board members have also to inspect the food of prisoners at frequent intervals. As food issues can be major sources of contention in prison, this is an important area. They can also enquire into a prisoner's mental or physical health and to check whether imprisonment is affecting his/her condition. Another important role is that of acting as an independent observer or witness in the event of a serious incident or disturbance in the prison. Members take up a wide range of prisoner and staff concerns during their visits and make their views known through a monthly meeting with the governor, an annual report to the Home Secretary, and, where appropriate, through the media.

Members perform an important role as a 'watchdog' or 'observer' body. As public representatives they have a significant part to play in overseeing the daily running of prisons, without being paid employees, or having any managerial involvement. The freedom which they have to visit any part of the prison gives them opportunity to listen to prisoners and staff in a unique way. At a time when prisons seem to becoming more punitive, in response to the political and public mood, the task laid before Boards is even more important. Issues of justice, fair treatment, and abuses need to be firmly held in focus. Many members act as a 'sounding-board' for staff, and they are able to challenge decisions and practices often taken for granted within the prison. Such challenges can only be a healthy contribution to reflection on role and belief.

> **Lord, we hold before you**
> **the work of members of**
> **Boards of Visitors.**
> **As they are entrusted**
> **with responsibility for**
> **inspecting prisons,**
> **may they do so with**
> **an eye for justice,**
> **a heart for those**
> **who have hurt,**
> **and may themselves be hurt;**
> **with an integrity**
> **which is for the**
> **common good.**

PRISON VISITORS ▦

WEEK on week in 107 prisons in England and Wales, men and women form relationships with prisoners, officially, and with the encouragement of the Home Office. At present there are 1,395 such visitors, 709 of whom are members of the National Association of Prison Visitors.

The relationships formed are about friendship between people of equal status—there can be no 'them and us'. Visitors see people, not 'problems' or 'prisoners'. They have a role in providing for the personal growth and development of people in prison. Prison visitors are all volunteers and they help provide a continuing link with the wider community, a listening ear, an opportunity for conversation which may rise above the immediacy of the prison context, and in which the value of each person is affirmed.

The history of prison visiting goes back as far as the beginnings of prison, but it is only in the last couple of centuries, with the development of prisons as we know them, that the work of prison visitors has taken its present course. People such as John Wesley, the father of Methodism, and Elizabeth Fry, Quaker and prison reformer, have been amongst the notable men and women involved.

Whilst in many prisons the chaplain acts as the Prison Visitor Liaison Officer, volunteers are selected on their ability to be good listeners and to carry on conversation, and not because of any religious interest they might have. People of all living-faith traditions, and none, are encouraged to apply.

Many prisoners have been grateful for the friendship offered, and received, by prison visitors and the value of such service is enormous for short as well as long-term prisoners.

Pam, a prison visitor for some years now, writes that this role 'can be exciting, exhilarating, and can leave one with a sense of fulfilment.

It can also be boring, frustrating and sometimes leaves me with a sense of failure. For a long time prior to starting as a visitor, I was interested in penal matters, but I have never been an idealist. Sometimes I think I am guilty of idealism, and I keep a constant check on it, reminding myself that I am a "visitor", and like all visitors, am "invited" in by the prisoner, to his home—the prison. If I had any ideas about being a "reformer", or I wanted to change the prison system, then I very definitely ought not to be a prison visitor.

'Over the last few years I have visited men whose crimes have been as different as their personalities and each time the challenge is the same—forming a friendship between two people who, under normal circumstances, would never have been brought together. Sometimes one is lucky—immediately we "click" and the conversation flows. At other times, though, it is uphill work and I feel we will never find enough in common to get the relationship off the ground. At other times, there is a breakthrough in what had been, up until then, an exchange of pleasant formalities.

'What I think I offer as a prison visitor is my weakness and my frailty, my vulnerability. A relationship based on vulnerability has little time for conventions. It is more real, more challenging, and sometimes more enjoyable. Maybe "enjoyment" is a key word in prison visiting and there is a very real pleasure in hearing a man bowed down with the weight of his crimes and his life in prison, laugh out loud with delight. There needs to be an acceptance of things as they are, here and now. We are not reformers, but transformers, though even that may be over-idealistic. We are there to offer the hand of friendship, sympathize (but never to say the patronizing, "I know just how you feel", as we don't, and we never will . . .), and, above all, to believe in someone who no longer believes in himself.'

Clothe yourselves with compassion, kindness, humility, meekness, and patience.   (Colossians 3: 12b)

God of compassion
you call us to
the difficult and joyful
task of friendship.

We give you thanks
for the gift of being
able to listen to other people,
and to you.

We pray for the work
of all prison visitors
as they seek to befriend,
to share, and to express
their care for prisoners.

Enable them,
in word and action
to express their belief
in the value of each person;
to affirm the dignity
and individuality
of those they serve,
and to be gracious
in generous listening.

INTERNATIONAL LINKS
AMONGST PRISON CHAPLAINS ▓

D URING recent years there has been increased awareness of the value of international links among prison chaplains. Many people are imprisoned in countries other than their native land, and the issues relating to imprisonment are similar in all countries.

Alan Duce, the Anglican chaplain at Lincoln Prison is the European Representative on the Steering Committee of the International Prison Chaplains Association. In the piece which follows, he helps to focus our thoughts and prayers on the benefits to be gained from chaplains co-operating across geographical divides.

Increasing numbers of prisoners in almost every country have become a focus of concern among Christians everywhere. This has led to more church people—both ordained and lay—taking up commissions to work as prison chaplains. Better communication among them encourages and invigorates them in their work and identity.

International links also counteract their isolation. Prison chaplains can often feel lonely. The general public does not readily warm to those who advocate compassion towards the offender and churches are sometimes less than wholehearted in their support for those who minister to the prisoner. Prisons for their part surround those who work in them with secluding walls.

Ministry to an increasing number of prisoners serving their sentences in prisons far from home has added to the significance of the international dimension to prison pastoral work. The importance of language, cultural identity and the creating of some initial links for a prisoner with a distant family possibly in strained political circumstances are recent aspects of prison ministry which add to the importance of building personal ministerial networks world-wide.

The benefits of international contacts were apparent to a group of eighty or so chaplains from almost every corner of the earth who attended the first International Consultation of Prison Chaplains at Bossey in Switzerland in August 1985. They came from diverse culture and contrasting prison regimes. For a week they sat together exchanging ideas in glorious sunshine beside Lake Geneva. They returned home exhilarated as a result of all they had shared.

At Bossey a decision was made to continue the spirit of that conference by forming the International Prison Chaplains' Association (IPCA). The affairs of the Association were initially conducted by four members of a European Steering Committee; at that time the roots of the Association lay among Protestants in northern Europe. The Vatican officially asked to join the Association in 1988. At the Second International Consultation of Prison Chaplains held again at Bossey in 1990, a new Steering Committee was created composed of ten people from all over the world including both Protestants and Catholics. The Third International Consultation was held in Ottawa in 1995 and the Fourth will possibly be held in Johannesburg in 2000.

IPCA has never had a political or profit-making motive, nor has it ever intended to become involved with penal policy or the affairs of prisoners in any country. IPCA has more positively been described as a 'movement' enabling all prison chaplains—not just those in prominent national positions—to link up with each other. The main purpose of the Association has been to foster dialogue at 'grass roots' level among prison chaplains.

The work of IPCA is to organize large five-yearly world conferences and to circulate regular world newsletters and prayer lists, as well as occasional international directories of prison chaplains. It also aims to set up regional branches of the Association to organize study groups in appropriate ways.

Heavenly Father
we hold before you the concern and compassion of all who
minister in your name in prisons throughout the world. Grant that
through the power of your Holy Spirit prison chaplains may feel
accompanied and supported by your presence in their work and

may all those committed to their spiritual care, both prisoners and staff, sense through their ministry your peace in their hearts. All this we ask through the grace of Jesus Christ our Lord.

PRISON FELLOWSHIP ▦

REMARKABLY, of the 134 prisons in England and Wales, 126 are supported by at least one Prison Fellowship Prayer Group, there being over 170 Prison Fellowship Groups. Prison Fellowship in England and Wales has 2,000 volunteers, of whom about 1,000 are actively involved in prison ministry, and is part of an international fellowship operating in over seventy countries, with an estimated 100,000 volunteers.

In England and Wales, it was started in 1979 by Sylvia Mary Alison, after considerable prayer and in response to a vision of God's work of renewal and re-formation of Church in the midst of the degradation, rejection, suffering, violence, and misery of our prison system. It defines itself as 'a body of Christian volunteers who, motivated by their love for God and in obedience to His commands, have joined together to exhort and assist His Church in prisons and in the wider community, in its ministry to prisoners, ex-prisoners, and their families, and to promote biblical standards of justice in the criminal justice system'.

Its aim is to befriend prisoners and their families, and to help them relate to God and to their neighbour. Basing itself on biblical foundations, it finds a gospel imperative based on three passages; in Mark 12: 31, where people are commanded to love their neighbour as themselves; in Luke 10: 25–37, where Christians are encouraged to imitate Jesus' concern for the outcasts in society; and in Matthew 5: 13–14, where we are encouraged to be salt and light in our communities. This is taken as an injunction to help to eliminate the causes of crime and to relieve the fear which it causes.

Prison Fellowship is rooted in, and for prayer. The aim is to envelope each prison establishment in prayer and in many action is also taken, as volunteer visitors, participants in groups, and as chaplains' assistants. It also seeks to help the families of prisoners, ex-prisoners, and their families within the community.

It is an ecumenical group and brings together Christians from many different denominational backgrounds and it exemplifies the potential to involve the ministry of the wider Church with the ministry of chaplains. That wider community must be involved in our prisons, and in the ministry of reconciliation.

I think that Pierre Allard, the Director of Chaplaincy Correctional Services in Canada has put this point extremely well: 'The myth that Chaplains can fulfil their ministry of reconciliation without the help of the larger faith community must be forever dispelled. However talented, however powerfully empowered by the Spirit, however strongly mandated by their churches, Chaplains must realize the communal dimension of the new covenant, and their own limitations in representing the outside community . . . Those who have experienced forgiveness from God must also experience forgiveness, acceptance, reconciliation from their brothers and sisters outside the walls. In the same vein, volunteers are not a nice addition or a passing fad. They are an integral part of the Chaplains' ministry.'

Prison Fellowship can make a significant contribution to all that Pierre Allard says.

> A bruised reed he will not break,
>   and a dimly burning wick he will not quench;
> he will faithfully bring forth justice.'
>
> (Isaiah 42: 3)

God our Father
we give you thanks
for the ministry of Prison Fellowship
in this country and abroad.
Encourage all who volunteer
to commit themselves
to love, which transforms,
to forgiveness, which heals,
to respect, which encourages,
to hope, which is grounded in you.

WELCOME THE STRANGER ▒

A s part of the preparation of people for release from prison, chaplains are sometimes able to commend a prisoner to a particular church and congregation. It is a difficult area for some churches, particularly, those regarded as being in the mainstream. Congregations are not always sure how to cope with the presence of a former prisoner.

The Reverend Tom Johns recounts a story about one man, to which I have added a prayer.

It was the Monday morning reception interviews in the Young Offender Institution. Bruce was a tall, well-built and impressive 18-year-old, who had a quiet confidence about him. He had been in prison before and he could almost give the answers before I asked the questions.

We were progressing along well until I asked him if he had any connections with the church outside. 'Funny you should say that,' he replied, 'last time I was in prison I was working in the gardens when an officer came and told me to change into my best kit because the Vicar had come to see me. I had never met my Vicar before but when we sat talking to each other we got on well.

'When I was discharged I thought, if the Vicar comes to see me I ought to go and see the Vicar. I had never been to church before so I put on my best jeans and T-shirt. I found it hard to go into church on my own but I managed to make my way to the back pew and waited for someone to come to me. Some ladies were talking and they looked at me but carried on speaking to each other.'

'Eventually, the service began. I would like to have joined in but no one gave me any books. I thought they would be pleased to see me but at the end of the service everyone went home and no one said a word to me.'

Bruce concluded by saying, 'There's more love in my criminal friends than in your Christian church.'

Subsequently, he reoffended and was given a long sentence. Maybe it would have been a different story had he found more love in the Christian Church than in his criminal friends.

. . . I was a stranger and you welcomed me.   (Matthew 25: 35b)

Lord, in your Son
you show us how you greet
the stranger and the outcast
with compassion.
As we seek to exercise
a ministry of welcome
in your name, we ask
for a spirit of acceptance
and tolerance which reflects
your love and grace
for all your people.

A PRISON LITANY ▦

L ITANY, as a form of intercessory prayer, has been part of Christian worship and devotion since at least the second half of the fourth century. It is a flexible and valuable way of encouraging effective congregational participation in the liturgy as well as comprehensively embracing areas for prayer. It is not, however, used as much as it might be.

The Reverend Tom Johns, currently an Assistant Chaplain General within the Prison Service Chaplaincy, and the Reverend John Tearnan, a former chaplain, have produced a Litany which reflects the intercessory needs of the prison context. It can be used as a whole, or in appropriate parts.

For the ministry that God has called us to among prisoners and members of staff, let us pray to the Lord.

God the Father,
have mercy on us.

God the Holy Spirit,
have mercy on us.

Holy, blessed and glorious Trinity whose unity draws us together,
have mercy on us.

From all evil and mischief; from pride, vanity and hypocrisy; from envy, hatred and malice, and from all evil intent,
good Lord deliver us.

From laziness, worldliness and love of money; from hardness of heart and contempt for your word and laws,
good Lord deliver us.

From the sins of body and mind; from all the deceits of the world, the flesh and the devil, and from anger and violence in word and deed, *good Lord deliver us.*

THE NEEDS OF THOSE INSIDE

For those in prison for the first time and for the families and friends from whom they are separated. Lord in your mercy
hear our prayer.

For those made hard and cynical by life in prison; for those who feel no sorrow for what they have done, and for those who are thinking of further crime. Lord in your mercy
hear our prayer.

For those who break the good order and discipline of prison life; for those in the segregation unit; and for those seeking protection. Lord in your mercy
hear our prayer.

For those who create anxiety and fear; for the weak who are abused by the strong; for those who desperately long to be accepted; for the unloved and the unwanted who receive neither letter or visit. Lord in your mercy
hear our prayer.

For those whose faith in Christ is mocked; for those who are taunted for going to Chapel, for reading the Bible and praying. For those who by their false and evil beliefs lead the simple away from the truth in Christ. Lord in your mercy
hear our prayer.

For those who stand firm in the faith and witness to Christ in word and in deed. Lord in your mercy
hear our prayer.

THE NEEDS OF THOSE OUTSIDE

For those who depend on alcohol to give them courage or to drown their misery, and for those whose lives and families have been destroyed through alcohol abuse. Lord, hear us.
Lord, graciously hear us.

For those who are addicted to drugs, and for those who sell them. Lord, hear us.
Lord, graciously hear us.

For those contemplating crime today; for those arrested and taken to the cells for the first time in their lives. Lord, hear us.
Lord, graciously hear us.

For those who advise the innocent to plead guilty; for those who have abandoned hope of a fair trial, and for those who are the victims of rough justice. Lord, hear us.
Lord, graciously hear us.

For the partners and families of prisoners as they suffer the 'second sentence', the loneliness of separation and the difficulties of visiting. Lord, hear us.
Lord, graciously hear us.

For those who are worried about the lack of money and the debts they have incurred. For those who deprive themselves for the benefit of their children and their partner in prison. Lord, hear us.
Lord, graciously hear us.

CHRISTIAN MINISTRY

For those who through word and deed bring true humanity to relationships and show compassion to the needs of others; let us bless the Lord.
Thanks be to God.

For those whose thoughts turn into prayer and whose prayer turns into action; let us bless the Lord.
Thanks be to God.

For all who show forth the gifts of the Spirit in love, joy, peace; for those who are patient, good, gentle, self-controlled and faithful; let us bless the Lord.
Thanks be to God.

For those whose love bears all things, hopes all things, endures all things, whose love never ends; let us bless the Lord.
Thanks be to God.

> *Lord, make us instruments of your peace.*
> *Where there is hatred, let us give your love.*
> *Where there is injury, pardon.*
> *Where there is doubt, faith.*
> *Where there is despair, hope.*
> *Where there is sadness, joy.*
> *Where there is darkness, light.*
>
> *For in giving we receive,*
> *in pardoning we are pardoned,*
> *and in dying we are born into eternal life.*

GLOSSARY ▨

This Glossary is intended to help readers understand some of the terms, expressions and prison slang used within the book. Some entries are not used within the text, but may be of interest to readers. It does not pretend to be exhaustive.

ABH Actual Bodily Harm

absconded failure to return from Temporary Release on Licence

adjudication internal disciplinary hearing by the governor, or one of his senior governors

administration the Department, headed by the Head of Management Services, which provides a wide range of support services to the establishment

adult offender any person sentenced to imprisonment and over the age of 21 years

allocation the decision about the prison appropriate to a particular prisoner

'A' man an inmate in Category A classification (see classification)

APVS Assisted Prison Visits Scheme, under which immediate relatives may have the cost of their visit paid, subject to their being on a sufficiently low income

association time when prisoners in closed establishments are not locked in their cells, but are free to mix with other prisoners on their landing, to watch television, or to play games

ACR Automatic Conditional Release, for prisoners serving twelve months to under four years. They are released automatically at the half-way point and are supervised until the three-quarters point of sentence (or to the very end in the case of some sex offenders), and will be '*at risk*' until the very end of the sentence should they commit a further imprisonable offence before the end of the original sentence. The court dealing with the new offence may add all or part of the outstanding sentence to any new sentence it imposes (*see* **AUR** and **DCR**)

AUR Automatic Unconditional Release. Prisoners serving less than 12 months are released automatically half-way through the sentence. No supervision applies, but they are '*at risk*' (see above) for the second half of the sentence

banged up, or **bang-up** prison slang for being locked in cell

bird prison slang for the length of a sentence

block prison slang for the Segregation Unit (*see* **Segregation Unit**)

C & R Control and Restraint, used for control purposes on individual prisoners

canteen prison shop, where prisoners can purchase certain items and goods

CC Confined to Cell

cell card card at the entrance to a cell, indicating the name, etc., of the occupant/s and their religious registration

censor officer designated to examine incoming and outgoing mail to ensure that it does not contain 'contraband', or break any other prison rule

Centre according to the size and complexity of a prison, and normally situated at ground level and in a central position, used as a regulating office for movement and control within the establishment.

CIT Construction Industry Training, provided for prisoners

civil prisoner person in prison for contempt of court, for debt, or for failure to comply with a court order (except an order to pay a fine on conviction), and for no other reason

classification, security:

1. **Category 'A'** those whose escape would be highly dangerous to the public, the police, or the security of the state
2. **Category 'B'** those for whom the highest conditions of security are not necessary, but for whom escape must be made very difficult
3. **Category 'C'** those who cannot be trusted in open conditions, but who are without the ability or resources to make a determined bid to escape

4. **Category 'D'** those who can be trusted not to escape in open conditions

These categories are based on a report by Lord Mountbatten on Prison Security, 1966.

CNA Certified Normal Accommodation—the number of prisoners that any establishment will hold without exceeding the number of places. In effect, it is the number of places in a prison, before overcrowding takes place

committal the process by which a court orders the detention of a person, whether convicted or not, in legal custody

control the maintenance of order within a prison. It should not be confused with security (*see security*)

control room sometimes known as the Communications Room, or Comms Room, it is a centre for information and the monitoring of prisoner movement. In times of emergency it may be used as the central point of control

CRO Criminal Record Office, which is situated in New Scotland Yard

Crown Court higher court, used for trying more serious criminal cases, hearing appeals from the Magistrates' Courts, and also for passing sentence on those cases referred by the Magistrates' Courts. The best known Crown Court is the Central Criminal Court— popularly known as the 'Old Bailey', and located in London

DCR Discretionary Conditional Release relates to prisoners serving four years or more. They become eligible for parole at the half-way point. They may be released on parole at any point between half-way and two-thirds. Release at two-thirds is automatic, but is on a licence that runs to the three-quarters point (or to the end for some sex offenders). They will be *'at risk'* (*see* **ACR**) until the end of their sentence

discharge grant a sum of money given to a prisoner at the time of release in order to help with the expenses of the first few days of release. A travel warrant to the person's place of abode is also issued. A slightly higher grant is given to those without a 'home' to go to

discipline office the section of management services which deals with all matters relating to prisoners' documentation and records

dispersal prisons closed and highly secure prisons holding convicted prisoners, including Category 'A' of standard, high, or exceptional risk status. There are currently six such prisons

ECHR European Court for Human Rights

ECR Emergency Control Room, to be found in all dispersal prisons; it contains communication and monitoring equipment and is staffed 24 hours a day

'E' man a prisoner who has shown, by actual escapes, or determined escape attempts, that he constitutes an escape risk is placed on the 'E' List. He is then subjected to increased observation, and wears a yellow 'strip' on his clothing, known as 'patches'

escort the officers who accompany a prisoner when he leaves the prison to attend a funeral, visit a sick relative, etc. Escort officers are responsible for the prisoners' safe custody

gander a capping device for the perimeter wall of a prison as part of its security

GBH Grievous Bodily Harm

ghosting prison slang for the transferring of a prisoner from one prison to another at very short notice

god, or **goad** refers to a prisoner placed in confinement, by the governor, under the provision of Rule 43 (or Rule 46 for young offenders), in the interests of 'good order and discipline'

Her Majesty's Pleasure a young person, under the age of 18 is detained at 'Her Majesty's Pleasure'. The Home Secretary currently decides the period of time

Inspectorate of Prisons an independent body, headed by Her Majesty's Inspector of Prisons, which inspects prisons, aspects of prison life and, at the Home Secretary's request, particular incidents. Reports are published

JR Judge's Remand, where a person is sentenced by the court to custody (or released on bail) pending the next stage of his trial, or the passing of sentence

knock-back prison slang for the unfavourable outcome of an adjudication, application for bail, or any request within the system

landing one of the 'floors' in a prison, often referred to simply by number, 'the ones', 'the twos', 'the threes', 'the fours'

landing officer one of the officers responsible for prisoners on a particular landing

licence document which authorizes the release of a prisoner before the end of his/her sentence, and sets out the conditions of release. Life sentence prisoners have a 'life licence'

local prison closed prison which receives prisoners from the courts on remand and under sentence. Servicing the courts, they are also responsible for the initial classification of prisoners. Some will also hold short-term convicted prisoners and may have a wing for young offenders, or for women

location prisoners' 'address' within the prison, e.g. C4.06, means the sixth cell on the fourth floor of 'C' Wing

Magistrate's Court lower court where the majority of cases are dealt with, and which forwards to the higher court (*see* **Crown Court**) on indictment more serious cases, as well as those which are thought to deserve a more severe penalty than the lower court can impose

mechanical restraints handcuffs, leather body-belts, and leather ankle straps, used with the written permission of the governor, and loose canvas dress, used with the written authority of the medical officer, for the control of violent prisoners, when absolutely necessary

MUFTI Minimum Use of Force Tactical Intervention. A system introduced in 1978 by which officers, wearing protective clothing, aim to control in a riot, or near riot, situation with the minimum amount of force required. (*see* **Control and Restraint**)

nonce prison slang for a sex offender

OCA Unit Observation, Classification, and Allocation Unit which exists in all local prisons to assess sentenced inmates

on report prisoner awaiting adjudication because he has been charged with an offence against internal discipline

OR prisoner segregated under the provision of Rule 43, at his 'own request' usually because he feels threatened by others because of the nature of his offence, or behaviour inside, e.g. grassing, failing to pay debts to a 'baron'

orderly trusted prisoner who works in areas such as the chapel (*See* **red-band**)

parole refers to release on licence (*see* **AUR**, **ACR**, and **DCR**)

PRES Pre Release Employment Scheme, whereby selected long-term and life-sentence prisoners may live in separate, hostel accommodation, outside the prison, from where they go out to work for outside employers

production 'delivery' of a prisoner to court for trial or sentence

protected room usually in the prison Healthcentre or Segregation Unit, this room has only built-in furniture, with flush internal surfaces to eliminate sharp edges, etc., or features which could be used as suspension points. In prison slang, 'the strip'

protective clothing unisex tunic and shorts made of untearable material

property prisoner's possessions, usually kept in the reception area

reception area where all new prisoners are 'received' into the prison; where they are bathed, medically examined, given their number, and provided with their prison clothing, etc. It is also a way of referring both to the process the newcomer undergoes ('he is on reception') and the newcomer himself ('there were five receptions last night')

reception board on the morning after reception, a board, which usually includes a governor grade, or Principal Officer, meet new receptions, verifying basic information about them and making initial decisions with regard to security category, and possibly, location. They also give information to the prisoner about practical matters of routine

reception letter letter issued on the day after reception so that a prisoner may write to a relative, friend, etc.

recidivist person who constantly re-offends and returns to prison

red-band prisoner trusted to work in areas such as the library, chapel, etc.

Remand Centre establishment, or a particular wing in a local prison, which accommodates those people, especially youngsters under 21 years of age, who are awaiting trial or, having been tried are awaiting sentence or allocation

RRLO Race Relations Liaison Officer. A member of staff, e.g. a governor, Principal or Senior Officer, who is deputed by the governor and trained by the Prison Service to act as the focal point for all race relations matters

Rule 43s prisoners segregated either because they are judged to be a serious threat to good order and discipline, or for the sake of their own protection, in accordance with Prison Rule 43 (*a*) and (*b*), respectively

screws prison slang for Prison Officers

search, rub-down light body search over the clothing

search, strip more thorough and intimate search of the person and clothing

security measures designed to prevent escapes from security. Also, those responsible for security

Security Officer senior member of staff holding responsibility for all aspects of security within a prison

Segregation (or Seg) Unit wing, or group of cells, isolated from the main prison accommodation, for the use of prisoners under punishment

SSU Special Secure Unit—a high-security unit within an already very secure prison

strip-cell *see* protected room

tally token, usually metal, given in exchange for keys and returned when keys are surrendered

throughcare care provided for an offender from the time of arrest until release, and afterwards

TOIL time off in lieu

TWOC taking (a vehicle) without the owner's consent

VFM value for money

VIR Viral Infectivity Restrictions: an indication of the presence of Hepatitis B, C, HIV positive, etc.

visit opportunity for a prisoner to be visited by a relative, friend, solicitor, etc.

visit closed where there is a clear partition of glass, reinforced plastic or wire-mesh between the prisoner and his visitor(s)

visit open where the prisoner is seated at a table, usually continuous, with relatives, etc., on the other side. Limited physical contact is possible

VO Visiting Order, or pass issued to a prisoner and sent to his relatives or friends allowing the admission of three visitors plus his children

vulnerable prisoners prisoners on Rule 43(*b*), or, in the case of a young offender, Rule 46

VPU Vulnerable Prisoner Unit. In some prisons this may be a special group of cells, or a separate unit, away from the main accommodation

weighed off prison slang meaning adjudicated by the governor

wing one of the main accommodation areas in a prison

young offender term used to cover all young prisoners under 21 years of age. Those who are 14 are known as children, those between 15 and 17, as young persons, and those between 17 and 21, as young adults

Young Offender Institution the Criminal Justice Act (1988) created a single custodial sentence for young offenders to be known as detention in a young offender institution

INDEX ▨

Who will separate us from the love of Christ?
Will hardship, or distress, or persecution, or famine, or
nakedness, or peril, or sword?

As it is written,
'For your sake we are being killed all day long;
we are accounted as sheep to be slaughtered.'

No, in all these things we are more than conquerors through
him who loved us. For I am convinced that neither death, nor
life, nor angels, nor rulers, nor things present, nor things to
come, nor powers, nor height, nor depth, nor anything else in
all creation, will be able to separate us from the love of God in
Christ Jesus our Lord.

(Romans 8: 35–9)